DO NOT REMOVE
CARDS FROM POCKET

10-17-94

ALLEN COUNTY PUBLIC LIBRARY
FORT WAYNE, INDIANA 46802

You may return this book to any agency, branch,
or bookmobile of the Allen County Public Library.

DEMCO

# MIGRANT FARM WORKERS

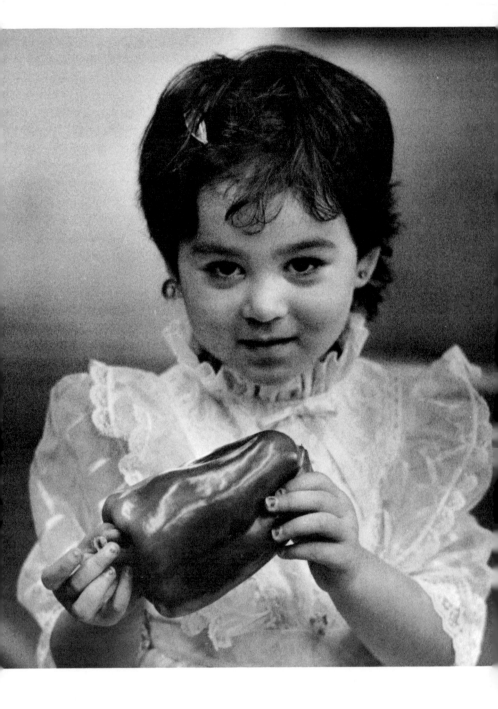

# MIGRANT FARM WORKERS

## THE TEMPORARY PEOPLE

by Linda Jacobs Altman

An Impact Book
Franklin Watts
New York  Chicago  London  Toronto  Sydney

Photographs copyright ©: Alan Pogue: pp. 2, 12, 54, 86, 89, 92, 93, 95, 99, 100; Library of Congress: p. 21; New York Public Library, Picture Collection: p. 23 top; FSA/Library of Congress: pp. 23 bottom, 24, 41, 52; U.S.D.A.: p. 30; Wide World Photos: pp. 32, 57, 75; Springer/Bettmann Film Archives: p. 36; UPI/Bettmann Newsphotos: pp. 46, 65, 97.

Library of Congress Cataloging-in-Publication Data

Altman, Linda Jacobs, 1943–
Migrant farm workers : the temporary people / by Linda Jacobs Altman.
p.    cm. —(An Impact book)
Includes bibliographical references and index.
ISBN 0-531-13033-9
1. Migrant agricultural laborers—United States—Juvenile literature.   2. Trade-unions—Migrant agricultural laborers—United States—Juvenile literature.   [1. Agricultural laborers. 2. Migrant labor.   3. United Farm Workers.]   I. Title.
HD1525.J33   1994
331.5′44′0975—dc20           93-11921   CIP   AC

# CONTENTS

# LIVING
# THE
# MIGRANT
# LIFE

The migrant life hasn't changed much over the years. Migrant farm workers never seem to belong in the "polite society" of those with steady jobs and permanent addresses.

As a group, migrant workers are irreplaceable in American agriculture. As individuals, they are unknown, part of that faceless mass of humanity called the farm work force.

Hidden under all the statistics regarding migrants are living, breathing human beings, trying to get by as best they can. With time and luck, some migrants escape the system, while others scratch out a living within it. Far too many become its victims.[1]

Among the latest to suffer under the present system are Mixtec Indians from the impoverished Mexican state of Oaxaca. They began pushing northward during the late eighties, bringing with them a whole set of new challenges for employers, social service agencies, and even their fellow migrants.

Many Mixtecs speak neither Spanish nor English but an ancient dialect of their own. They fled the grinding poverty of their lives in southern Mexico, made their way across a border they weren't supposed to cross, and undercut more experienced migrants by working for less money and living under worse conditions.[2]

Like many Mixtecs, Salvador and Juanita had heard stories of plentiful work and good pay on American farms. Leaving their two children behind with Juanita's mother, the young couple headed north. They paid four hundred dollars to a "coyote" (independent labor contractor) to smuggle them both across the border.

After a frightening ride in a dark and stuffy van, Salvador and Juanita arrived in what was to them a kind of promised land. Juanita was eight months pregnant at the time.

Though Juanita was willing to work, no American grower was willing to hire a woman who was so far along in her pregnancy, so Salvador looked for a job. With no money and no contacts, the couple lived in a dark, damp little cave north of San Diego. Other illegals from Oaxaca joined them there.

Finally, Salvador found work in the tomato harvest near Madera. He and Juanita left the cave behind, but that didn't mean they found better accommodations. Instead of a cave, they lived in an old, beat-up station wagon, paying a fellow worker fifteen dollars a week to park in his driveway and use his water faucet.

Salvador earned thirty-five cents for every five-gallon bucket he filled. By starting at three-thirty in the morning and working as fast as humanly possibly, he sometimes managed to fill two hundred buckets in a day. His big ambition was to save enough money to rent a room so Juanita would have heat, running water, and a toilet after the baby was born. The birth itself would take place in the car, with the help of a friend from home.

The day-to-day realities of migrant experience sometimes take strange, even violent, turns as workers find themselves at odds with local populations. Often it takes very little to turn suspicion into confrontation or even into outright violence.

In an affluent town near San Diego, vigilantes raided

a migrant campsite after a local woman was assaulted by Hispanics. The brutal beatings put three migrant farm workers in the hospital and left law enforcement officers wary of what might happen next.[3]

Farther north, the owners of a small but productive walnut grove hired migrants for the autumn harvest and gave them permission to camp near a small creek that ran through the property.

The migrant camp was nothing like what the owners expected it to be—neat and clean, with green canvas tents set up in orderly rows. Instead, people lived out of rattletrap cars and scattered trash everywhere.

Then the stealing began. The owners were afraid to leave their homes unattended; something would always disappear. By the end of that harvest, they had vowed never again to allow "those people" to stay on the property.

Did the workers steal from their employer? Quite possibly some of them did, but it's unlikely that *all* of them did. The owners didn't care about questions of guilt or innocence. From their point of view, "those people" had ruined one season. They wouldn't get a chance to ruin another. Next time workers arrive to pick a crop, they'll find NO CAMPING signs posted all over the property. The innocent suffer right along with the guilty, and rarely does anyone have recourse against the system. Migrants who break the rules face swift and often harsh punishment. Those who use the rules to stand up for their own rights risk reprisals.

In October 1990, Luis Hernandez and twenty-three other Mexican farm workers were finishing the peach season near the northern California town of Yuba City. Conditions in the company-run labor camp were so terrible that Mexican Consul Nicolas Escalante helped them alert local health authorities.

The next April, when Luis and the others reported to

9

begin another season's work, the infuriated owner not only fired them but confiscated their belongings and locked them out of their camp. The desperate workers sought help from California Rural Legal Assistance. They told CRLA attorney Ilene Jacobs a long and often unnerving story of intimidation and abuse; of the owner's driving through camp firing a 12-gauge shotgun into the air, pounding one worker's car with a hammer, and nailing washroom doors shut.

At that prosperous orchard, health department investigators found people living in a burned-out shell of an old house. They slept on filthy mattresses, which were often laid on top of exposed electrical wires. Nineteen people shared one bathroom.

Under provisions of a seldom-used federal law, a U.S. district judge ordered the grower to repair the camp and rehire the workers.

When Luis Hernandez and the others who stood with him won their case for decent housing and fair employment practices, they scored a small but important victory for migrant workers. Unfortunately, it was also a rare victory.

The very mobility of the agricultural labor force works against reform. The government passes laws it can't consistently enforce, and in the final analysis the workers are left to struggle with their own problems in their own way.

In south Texas, longtime migrants have challenged the odds to create one of the most stable farm worker communities in the country. Though the people travel for more than half the year, they maintain permanent homes in one of the numerous *colonias* that dot the rural landscape of the Rio Grande Valley. These informal settlements house the poorest of the poor, often in dirt-floor shacks without indoor plumbing or a safe supply of drinking water.[4]

Refugio and Maria Valdez don't worry about such nice-
ties; simply having a place to call their own is enough.
They are both in their forties, with work-hardened hands
and faces lined from hours of working in the sun. Maria
has borne eight children, six of whom are still alive.
Though she is a grandmother several times over, she still
has a ten-year-old at home.

For more than half of every year, the Valdez family
travels with a group of relatives and friends, working the
crops up and down the heartland of America. In the off-
season, they return to the colonia to pick up the fabric of
their lives.

Refugio and Maria take great pride in their little
house. Though it has only two rooms, with a small kitchen
and no indoor plumbing, Maria keeps it scrupulously
clean. Refugio loves to fix up the yard with brightly
colored plaster statues, decorative stones, and cactus
plants. Lavishing love and attention upon their little house
is as close as Refugio and Maria Valdez can get to the
kind of stable home life others take for granted.

In California, another farm worker family pursues its own
dream of permanence. Juan and Celia Gonzales were
luckier than most; after years of traveling throughout the
state of California, picking dates in Indio, lettuce in Salinas,
and pears in Kelseyville, Juan landed a year-round job
tending vineyards in the California wine country. The family
moved into a small house. It was a run-down little place,
far too small for two parents, four kids, one grandmother,
and an occasional widowed aunt. That didn't matter.

The house was a dream come true. Never mind that
the roof leaked when it rained and the toilet didn't flush
exactly right. For the first time in their lives, the Gonzales
family had a home. They also had a car that hadn't broken
down for six whole months, an honest-to-goodness ad-

*The idea of a permanent place to live is a far-off dream for most migrant farm workers, who live instead in temporary dirt-floor shelters.*

dress where they could get mail sent to somebody besides "occupant," and enough food so nobody had to go hungry.

To fifteen-year-old Danny Gonzales, the best part was getting to stay in one school for a whole term. Following the crops meant you were always the new kid in class. Nobody paid much attention to you. Why bother? Migrants never stayed for long.

In his latest school, Danny is beginning to make decent grades. His guidance counselor is already talking about college. Danny isn't quite sure what he wants, but he is absolutely certain of what he *doesn't* want; a life of toiling in the fields as a migrant farm worker.

Farm work is by nature grueling, and even the best labor camps are cheerless places with few of the comforts most of us have grown to expect. It has been this way from the very beginning. Like all other people in all other walks of life, each migrant is a unique human being with a story all his own. Beneath those separate stories there is a common history that unites modern migrants with one another and with the countless thousands who have preceded them in the fields and orchards of the land.

# EARLY HISTORY AND ECONOMICS OF MIGRANT LABOR

According to the dictionary, *migrate* means to move from one region to another with the change of seasons. Though this definition is factual, it doesn't begin to describe life for thousands of migrant laborers who move from farm to farm and crop to crop, picking the harvest of other people's fields. The modern migrant lives on the fringes of a society that values settled lives, steady jobs, and more or less permanent homes. He is a stranger everywhere he goes; he can't stay long enough to become anything else.

## PREHISTORIC MIGRANTS

Thousands of years in the human past, everyone was a migrant. People had not learned to grow their own food, so they had no choice but to move through the countryside, following the herds of game animals and foraging for edible plants along the way.

In his book *Man Makes Himself*, anthropologist V. Gordon Childe gives an idea of the skills these early hunter-gatherers had to learn in order to survive:

> *Success in hunting could only be attained by prolonged and accurate observation of the habits of game; the results must have been built up into a collective tradition of hunting lore. The distinction between nutritive*

*and poisonous plants again had presumably to be learned by experience, and once more incorporated into a common tradition. . . . Man must learn the right seasons for hunting the different species of game or collecting the several kinds of eggs and fruits. To do so successfully he must eventually decipher the calendar of the heavens; he must observe the phases of the moon and the risings of stars, and compare these observations with the botanical and zoological ones already mentioned.*[1]

In time, this knowledge of where and how to find food expanded into what has been called the *agricultural revolution*. Humankind learned to plant, cultivate, harvest, and store food, thereby taking control of the food supply. For the first time in history, people no longer had to keep moving in order to survive.

In regions of fertile soil and plentiful rain, former migrants established settlements that grew into villages, townships, and cities. Ownership of land, which had been unthinkable to nomadic hunter-gatherers, became a necessity to settled agriculturalists. People began to define themselves in terms of property, with the wealthiest being those who owned the most land, while the poorest were those who owned the least. The remaining migrants, who owned no land at all, became perpetual outsiders. Their way of life survives today among such wandering tribes as the bedouin of the Sahara and the Bushmen of the deep Kalahari.

## NEW WORLD MIGRANTS

Many Native Americans lived in nomadic tribes, following buffalo herds over the vast grasslands of the central plains. The arrival of European settlers slowly pushed the buffalo to the edge of extinction and the Indians onto reservations where they were no longer free to roam.

16

The America settled by Europeans began as a country of farmers. In the first census, taken in 1790, the new nation had a population of 3,929,000, only 202,000 of whom lived in towns of 2,500 or more. The rest lived on farms or in small rural settlements where everybody grew his own garden, kept a few chickens for eggs and meat, and had a cow for milk, butter, and cheese.

In New England, the small, family-sized farm dominated the economy. Secretary of Treasury Albert Gallatin chose the town of Ridgefield, Connecticut, for his 1810 report on typical settlements. Ridgefield was home to about two hundred farm families, who bought few products outside their homes. They grew their own food, made their own soap, candles, carpets, and clothes. As they planted only enough for their own needs, and perhaps a small surplus for bartering with neighbors, the farmers of New England had limited need for migrant workers to harvest their fields.

The migrants of early New England were not farmhands but itinerant craftsmen such as tanners, tinkers, and shoemakers, who offered services not easily performed by untrained family members. These tradesmen often traveled alone, living and working in their horse-drawn wagons. Though they had no permanent homes, they were not "poor migrants" to the people they served. They were "free spirits" whose possession of a valued trade made them welcome everywhere they went.

The self-reliant small farmer did not dominate in the South as he did in New England. Ownership of southern land was determined by a *headright system*: each farmer who came to settle in America could have fifty acres for himself and fifty for each person he brought over. This arrangement led to holdings far larger than any one family could handle and thus to an early development of *cash-crop agriculture*—crops raised primarily for sale rather than for a family's own use. The invention of the cotton gin in 1793 made cotton ideal for this kind of farming.

Other suitable crops were sugar, rice, wheat, and corn. These mass-production crops needed mass-production labor, and so cash-crop agriculture brought America's first farm labor shortages. There was not yet a readily available pool of migrant farm labor, and so southern plantation owners turned to slavery as an answer to their labor problems. The personal misery and social upheaval resulting from that decision are well-documented facts of American history.

When slavery finally ended, it was not a vast and mobile labor force that took its place; it was sharecropping. The croppers, as they were called, were mostly former slaves who farmed a small plot of land, growing whatever the landlord told them to grow. At harvest time, the cropper paid rent in the form of a portion of his crop. In return, he received a shack to live in, a small space where he could grow vegetables for his own use, and the proceeds form his share of the cash crop.

As America expanded westward, thousands of unskilled laborers came as refugees from various disasters in their homelands. In 1846, for example, blight destroyed Ireland's entire potato crop, causing widespread famine. Desperate Irishmen came to America rather than face slow starvation at home. "The jobs that Irish immigrants held were not simply hard, dirty and dangerous," writes historian Thomas Sowell. "They were also unsteady, as unskilled work often was and is. Once a canal or railroad had been built, the workers were out of a job. The same was true of many other construction jobs, seasonal work, and casual occupations."[2]

Some of these workers became the core of a migrant farm labor force. Others took advantage of the Homestead Act of 1862. This law opened the Great Plains by permitting any white citizen or immigrant alien of sound mind and body to file for 160 acres. He had only to clear the land and cultivate it to receive title from the government.

18

Hundreds of people rushed to claim their share of t
American Dream. Some succeeded in building a life fur
themselves. Others ended up borrowing to make it
through one lean season after another, then losing everything when they couldn't repay the loans. Many of these
bankrupt homesteaders stayed to become tenant farmers
on land they once owned. Others took to the road, finding
farmwork wherever and however they could.

By 1900 migrants had settled into a pattern, following
the harvest from Texas in June to the Dakotas and Montana in September. These midwestern migrants were single men rather than family groups. They were called
hoboes, and they became the focus of countless legends
and tall tales. Settled folk romanticized their tattered
clothing, their "hobo jungle" encampments, their free-
wheeling, wandering ways. Because hoboes were neces-
sary to the harvest, farmers welcomed them and railroad
detectives looked the other way when hoboes caught free
rides on passing freight trains.

According to agricultural historian John T. Schlebecker, hoboes didn't become unpopular until 1911,
when the invention of the combine made them unneces-
sary to the midwestern grain harvest.[3] After that, these
"knights of the road," as they were sometimes called,
became plain old bums in the eyes of farmers, townsfolk,
and railroad officials.

## PACIFIC COAST MIGRANTS

California agriculture developed differently from that of
the East and Midwest. When California was part of Mexico, huge Spanish land grants put it under the control
of a few aristocratic families. When wealthy Americans
began to buy out the Spanish, the names on the deeds
changed but the size of the holdings did not. The land
remained in the hands of a wealthy few. These vast em-

pires lent themselves to large-scale, cash-crop agriculture.

The gold rush of 1849 brought an influx of people eager to strike it rich in the mines. When the gold played out, some of those people went home, some worked on the railroad, helping to lay the first coast-to-coast track, and some drifted from one place to another, taking whatever jobs they could find. In 1869, the transcontinental railroad was completed, and hundreds of workers joined the ranks of California's unemployed. These former miners and railroad workers formed a core group of migrants just when technological advances were opening new markets for California growers.

In the same year the transcontinental line was completed, the first refrigerated railroad car carried a shipment of bananas from California to Chicago, proving that even perishable fruits and vegetables could now be shipped all over the country. At the same time, the canning industry was growing into a major market for produce that could be processed, canned, and stored almost indefinitely. Together, refrigeration and canning brought sweeping changes in mass-market agriculture. Fruits and vegetables that had once been too perishable to grow in commercial quantities now became profitable, and California fields abounded with everything from asparagus to zucchini.

These garden crops were more difficult to harvest than wheat, barley, and other staples. Most had to be handpicked, which meant that growers needed a reliable source of cheap, plentiful labor during every harvest season. They wanted workers who would show up when needed and disappear when the work was done. Thus began the cycle that saw one ethnic group after another brought to work on California's farms.

In his book *Factories in the Fields*, Carey McWilliams described the situation in California: "The practice has been to use a race for a purpose and then to kick it

*Although Chinese immigrants were initially welcomed into the migrant labor force, feelings of resentment spread as their numbers grew.*

out, in preference for some weaker racial unit. In each instance, the shift in racial units has been accompanied by a determined effort to drive the offending race from the scene.''[4]

The Chinese were the first group tapped by California growers. In the 1850s many were employed mining gold or laying railroad track, but by 1869 the gold boom was over, the transcontinental railroad was finished, and the Chinese turned to agriculture. In 1870 they made up only one-tenth of the migrant work force. By 1880 they accounted for more than half.

As soon as the Chinese became a sizable presence in California, the backlash against them began. When the Chinese Exclusion Act of 1882 put an end to new immigration, resentful Anglos turned their attention to the Chinese who were already in the country. According to historian Ruthanne Lum McCunn, "Feelings against the Chinese grew so strong that it was dangerous for them to remain in the countryside. Many of the large ranchers and farmers watched their farms, factories and vineyards go up in flames, forcing them to get rid of their Chinese workers."[5]

The Japanese were next to be tapped for California's migrant work force. Between 1890 and 1910 their number grew from 2,000 to over 100,000. The typical Japanese immigrants were ambitious young men from farming backgrounds, who were neither terribly poor nor especially rich. They approached migrant farm work in a businesslike manner, forming "clubs" or "associations," and designating one member to locate jobs and direct work in the fields. These group leaders, usually called "secretaries," made hiring more efficient for the growers, who had to deal with only one man to hire dozens. The secretary had full authority to represent the group to the outside world, but in the fields he was not a "boss." He was a coordinator who saw to it that the crew worked without wasted motion or duplication of effort.

In 1910, a revolution in Mexico began to change the migrant labor force in California, as hundreds of impoverished peasants flocked northward to seek work. This influx of Mexicans was supplemented by the so-called tide of turbans, in which hundreds of Sikhs from India entered the United States by way of Canada. Other groups that

*Many new arrivals from around the world, such as this Greek woman (left) or this group of Filipino boys thinning lettuce (below), began to fill the ranks of the migrant farm labor force.*

*Mexican nationals soon came to be favored by
growers, since many returned home after each
season and thus did not create problems such
as housing shortages or unemployment, which
were often presented by domestic farm workers.*

came to work in California included Italians and Arme-
nians. Of all these new arrivals, the Mexicans quickly
became most popular with California farmers. They came
when they were needed and left when they were through.
Others, being far away from their homelands, had no-

where to go when the season ended and so were often seen as a drain on local resources. As the favored group, Mexicans soon came to dominate the migrant work force to such an extent that growers feared critical labor shortages if Mexican immigration should ever be curtailed. To guard against such an occurrence, grower associations sent recruiters to the Philippine Islands. At that time, the Philippines was a United States territory, and its nationals therefore had an unrestricted right to enter this country. In 1923, 2,426 Filipinos took advantage of that right. The number climbed each year, peaking in 1929, with 5,795 workers.

With the addition of the Filipinos to the ethnic mix in California's fields, the migrant work force finally seemed to be large enough and mobile enough to meet the growers' needs.

As the decade of the twenties came to an end, California was firmly committed to maintaining the large and mobile seasonal work force that made mass-market farming profitable. The rest of the country clung to older ways, with smaller, family-sized farms worked by homesteaders, tenants, and sharecroppers. American agriculture as a whole seemed prosperous and healthy with migrant farm workers an important but relatively small part of the overall picture.

# MIGRANT
# LABOR
# AND THE
# GREAT
# DEPRESSION

The Great Depression began on October 24, 1929, when the stock market crashed, bankrupting many an investor and sending the entire economy into a tailspin that hit its low point in the spring of 1933. By March of that year, over fourteen million people were out of work, and those who did keep their jobs often had to take large pay cuts. Thousands of mortgages went into foreclosure, and thousands lost their savings as 3,377 banks closed their doors.

The downward spiral hurt farms as well as banks and businesses. By 1932, farm prices had fallen 50 percent below their 1929 levels as canneries stopped production and food wholesalers found that grocers couldn't afford to stock what their jobless customers couldn't afford to buy.

All across the country families cut their food buying to a minimum subsistence level. Meat, eggs, milk products, and fresh produce spoiled in the grocery markets; canned or otherwise processed foods accumulated in warehouses; and nonfood crops like cotton and tobacco built up huge surpluses. Prices fell so low that farmers couldn't earn enough from the sale of their crops to pay the cost of harvest. In February of 1932, a Congressional committee heard testimony about acres of wheat left uncut in Montana fields, apples rotting in the orchards of Oregon. Crops in every part of the country were abandoned by the ton.

## FROM SHARECROPPER TO MIGRANT

In spring of 1933, President Franklin D. Roosevelt gave the agricultural crisis a top priority in his new administration. Roosevelt was inaugurated on March 4, 1933, and by May 12, he had pushed the Agricultural Adjustment Act through Congress. A new government agency, the Agricultural Adjustment Administration (AAA), was formed to implement the law.

AAA aimed to stabilize prices and reduce farm surpluses through a complicated crop-reduction program and a system of loans and outright subsidies to put money into the hands of farmers. The agency chose southern cotton as the first target for crop reduction.

Forty million acres of cotton had already been planted by the time the Agricultural Adjustment Act went into effect, and the fields promised a bumper crop of cotton that nobody needed or wanted or could afford to buy. Warehouses bulged with eight million bales of surplus cotton from previous years, so the AAA began recruiting farmers in the Cotton Belt states of the Deep South— Mississippi, Alabama, Georgia, Louisiana—to participate in a cotton plow-up program.

These farmers agreed to plow up some ten million acres of newly planted cotton in return for over a hundred million dollars in benefit payments. In signing up participants for crop reduction the AAA defined ''farmer'' as ''landowner,'' making no provisions at all for the thousands of sharecroppers who had worked the fields of the South since the end of slavery. Because of this, the crop-reduction program that saved the price of cotton and the assets of many landowners also displaced hundreds of

27

sharecropping families—most of them black, some of them white, all of them poor.

Frederick Lewis Allen described the situation in *Since Yesterday*:

> *How easy for an owner of farm property, when the government offered him a check for reducing his acreage in production, to throw out some of his . . . sharecroppers, buy a tractor with the check, and run his farm mechanically with the aid of hired labor—not the sort of year-round hired labor which the old-time "hired man" had represented, but labor engaged only by the day when there happened to be work to be done.*[1]

After the cotton plow-up program, these day laborers were often as not displaced sharecroppers who traveled from farm to farm, seeking whatever work they could find. Thus the AAA's narrow view of farming threw hundreds of impoverished families into a migrant work force that fanned out in every direction. In time, some migrants traveled the entire eastern seaboard, following the harvest from the citrus groves of southern Florida to the potato fields of Long Island, New York. Others stayed closer to home, hiring themselves out to local farmers at peak seasons, while still others headed for the cities, where they often became an additional drain on already overburdened social services. In his book *The Great Depression*, David A. Shannon discusses the plight of the new wanderers:

> *Americans have always been a footloose people, but the Great Depression created a new kind of wanderer, the poverty-stricken nomad seeking escape from an intolerable life at home. Optimism had been a*

28

*characteristic of earlier wanderers, the colonist, the immigrant, the westward-trekking farmer, the gold seeker. . . . Desperation, not optimism, was the main characteristic of the nomads of the 1930's.*[2]

A 1935 Supreme Court ruling in the case of *United States* v. *Butler* found the Agricultural Adjustment Act to be unconstitutional. A stopgap measure, the Soil Conservation and Domestic Allotment Act, passed in February 1936; by 1938, Congress had formulated another, more acceptable, version of the Agricultural Adjustment Act. These later measures offered some protection to those sharecroppers who remained on their land, by requiring owners to keep the same number of sharecropper dwellings they'd had in 1933. By the time this provision went into effect, hundreds of sharecroppers had already joined the swelling ranks of migrant farm workers.

## FROM TENANT FARMER TO MIGRANT

Farmers in the Midwest had to contend with natural disaster as well as economic upheaval. The Great Plains, which consists of parts of the Dakotas, Montana, Nebraska, Wyoming, Kansas, Colorado, Oklahoma, Texas, and New Mexico had always been subject to high winds and recurring droughts. In 1930, while depression was taking hold of the economy, drought hit the plains. Three years of scant rainfall were followed by a season of dust storms worse than any the farmers had seen.

The first of these "great black blizzards" hit South Dakota on November 11, 1933. By the next day, the dust cloud over South Dakota was visible in Chicago. The day after that, it darkened skies as far away as Albany, New York. Journalist R. D. Lusk described that first storm in the *Saturday Evening Post*:

After three years of drought and a series of violent dust storms had left the fertile Great Plains barren, many farmers took to the roads in search of whatever work could be found.

By mid-morning, a gale was blowing, cold and black. By noon it was blacker than night, because one can see through night and this was an opaque black. It was a wall of dirt one's eyes could not penetrate, but it could penetrate the eyes and ears and nose. It could penetrate to the lungs until one coughed up

*black. . . . When the wind died and the sun shone*
*forth again, it was a different world. There were no*
*fields, only sand drifting into mounds and eddies. . . .*
*In the farmyard, fences, machinery, and trees were*
*gone, buried. . . . The roofs of sheds stuck out*
*through drifts deeper than a man is tall.*[3]

So it began, and the storms continued, one after another.
The Dust Bowl, as it came to be called, wasn't an entirely
natural disaster; droughts and heat and high winds come
from nature, to be sure, but human beings had overculti-
vated the land. James D. Horan sums up the situation in
*The Desperate Years*:

> *In the beginning, the Great Plains had been a sea*
> *of grass, first for the buffalo, then for the cattle barons.*
> *Before the end of the [nineteenth] century the range*
> *had been badly damaged by overgrazing. Then came*
> *the sodbusters . . . who tried to cultivate their 160*
> *acre plots. The world was crying for wheat after World*
> *War I, and the land was torn up to supply the demand.*[4]

The dust storms that began in 1933 buried the crops in
the fields and then stripped the fertile topsoil from the
barren land. The AAA stepped in to implement principles
of soil conservation and crop rotation in an effort to re-
claim the land. These methods required land-use planning
over a wide area, and so the patchwork of small family
farms, each operated independently of all the others, became outmoded. Landowners began to consolidate their
holdings, using federal relief funds received from AAA
to buy tractors and other modern equipment so they could
combine hundreds of small family farms into a few
"megafarms." Neither the tenant farmer nor the small
homesteader fit into the new scheme of things. These
people had little choice but to leave the land.

*Many drought refugees, who came to be known as "Okies," migrated to California to find profitable farm work, but instead received very low pay and lived in squalid camps, called "Hoovervilles."*

## THE GREAT MIGRATION

Whole families of former tenant farmers packed their belongings into ancient jalopies and left the prairie behind them. They were joined by homesteaders who'd sold out and even by former sharecroppers from the South who had not been able to sustain themselves working on East Coast farms. As all these landless workers massed on the Great Plains, growers in California saw the opportunity

32

to tap a vast source of cheap field labor. They circulated handbills, offering plenty of work at good wages. People read the flyers and heard the rumors of good weather, good work, and good living conditions, and headed for California.

"They roll westward like a parade," wrote journalist Richard L. Neuberger. "In a single hour from a grassy meadow near an Idaho road I counted thirty-four automobiles with the license plates of states between Chicago and the [Rocky] mountains."[5]

By 1935, a survey of seven counties in southeastern Colorado showed 2,811 farmhouses newly abandoned and only 2,878 still occupied.[6] The total number of refugees who entered California during the Dust Bowl years has been estimated by the U.S. Department of Labor at 350,000. So many of those refugees came from Oklahoma that the name Okies was applied to all. Actually, they came from all over the Midwest and the South; cotton pickers, dirt farmers, people with nowhere else to go and nothing left to lose. In his classic novel *The Grapes of Wrath*, John Steinbeck captured the hopes and fears of thousands in one poignant scene with his fictional Joad family:

> *[Ma Joad] filled up her bucket with hot water from the stove, and she put in dirty clothes and began punching them down into the soapy water. . . . "I like to think how nice it's gonna be, maybe, in California. Never cold. An' fruit ever'place, an' people just bein' in the nicest places, little white houses in among the orange trees. I wonder—that is, if we all get jobs an' all work—maybe we can get one of them little white houses. An' the little fellas go out an' pick oranges right off the trees. . . ."*
>
> *Tom watched her working, and his eyes smiled. "I knowed a fella from California . . . he says they's too many folks lookin' for work right there now. An'*

*he says the folks that pick the fruit live in dirty ol'*
*camps an' don't hardly get enough to eat. He says*
*wages is low an' hard to get any."*

*A shadow crossed her face. "Oh, that ain't so,"*
*she said. "Your father got a han' bill on yella paper,*
*tellin' how they need folks to work. Costs 'em good*
*money to get them han' bills out. What'd they want to*
*lie for, an' costin 'em money to lie?"*

*Tom shook his head. "I don't know, Ma. It's*
*kinda hard to think why they done it. Maybe . . ." He*
*looked out at the hot sun, shining on the red earth.*

*"Maybe what?"*

*"Maybe it's nice, like you says . . ."*[7]

## NEW MIGRANTS IN CALIFORNIA

So many refugees poured into California that there simply
wasn't enough work, enough food, enough housing to go
around. As farmers without land, the migrant laborers
roamed up and down the state, competing with others like
themselves for a few days' work. The lucky ones who
found jobs often lived in cramped and dirty labor camps
run by the employer. The "cabins" were tiny, one-room
shacks, many with no heat, indoor plumbing, or electric-
ity. Even these pitiful quarters lasted only as long as the
job itself. When the harvest was over, the workers had
to get out as quickly and quietly as possible.

During periods of unemployment (which were fre-
quent and often lengthy), dozens of migrant farm workers
crowded together in impromptu shantytowns made out of
whatever castaways lay at hand: everything from card-
board and old newspapers to the dented remains of old
jalopies might serve as part of a crude shelter. Someone
with a fine sense of irony dubbed these appalling settlements Hoovervilles after Herbert Hoover, the former
president, whom many blamed for the Depression. Local
people despised these Hoovervilles as breeding places of

34

crime and disease. Periodically, law enforcement authorities or vigilante groups would run the refugees off and burn down settlements.

The government established some camps for migrant farm workers, offering decent sanitation facilities and a respite from the horrors of Hoovervilles. The fictional facility that sheltered the Joad family in *The Grapes of Wrath* was based on an actual federal camp near Arvin, California.

Even when there was fieldwork to do, the pay was so low that a migrant family would have to work all day just to buy groceries for a single meal. There were so many migrant farm workers competing for jobs that growers could keep wages low and still get all the workers they needed. To ease this oversupply of labor, the government decided to stop foreign nationals from coming into the country to work on American farms. In practice, this meant restricting immigration from Mexico and the Philippines, the two countries that had furnished a large portion of California's pre-Depression migrant work force. The border patrol tightened security at the Mexican border, and Congress passed a law on July 11, 1935, which provided free transportation home for those Filipinos who were willing to leave the United States. As the Philippines was no longer a U.S. territory, having gained transitional independence on March 24, 1934, Congress could legally prohibit further immigration from the islands.

The banishment of foreign labor scarcely made a dent in the problem. There were still more migrant farm workers than jobs, so employers could keep wages low. To further complicate the situation, the prices of California's agricultural products fell so low that many crops went to waste. Throughout the state, growers chose to destroy their crops rather than sell at a loss so heavy that the cost of harvest could drive them to bankruptcy. To them, it was a matter of economic survival, as it had been to the

*The epic film*
The Grapes of Wrath,
*based on John Steinbeck's
stirring novel, dramatized
the plight of Dust Bowl
refugees.*

southern cotton growers who participated in the 1933
plow-up program. John Steinbeck's account of the farm
workers' feelings makes a moving summation to the saga
of the Okies in California:

> *The works of the roots of the vines, of the trees,
> must be destroyed to keep up the price, and this is the
> saddest, bitterest thing of all. . . . There is a sorrow
> here that weeping cannot symbolize. There is a failure
> here that topples all our success . . . and in the eyes of
> the people the grapes of wrath are filling and growing
> heavy, growing heavy for the vintage.*[8]

# MIGRANTS AND THE NEW AGRICULTURE

Everybody feared what would happen if that wrath ever broke loose. The migrant farm labor force was so huge, so unstable and unwieldy that nobody quite knew what to do about it. Government, organized labor, and social service providers chose to regard migrant farm workers as victims of a temporary problem rather than members of a permanent, though fluid work force. This attitude sealed the migrants' fate for many years to come by making it possible for government to ignore them in planning benefits for permanent, full-time workers in business and industry.

A major part of President Roosevelt's "New Deal" legislation dealt with labor relations. In 1935 alone, the Wagner Act gave workers the right to form unions and engage in collective bargaining through those unions, while the Social Security Act provided benefits for their old age. Both of these laws excluded migrant farm workers. Their sheer numbers would have bankrupted the system before it got off the ground, or so opponents claimed. Besides, the Depression would end, the Okies would land steady jobs, the small migrant force that remained would go back to doing what it had always done, and the migrant problem would simply disappear.

It didn't work out that way. The consolidated superfarms of the South and Midwest needed a steady supply of migrant laborers to replace the lost tenants and sharecroppers at times of peak need. California growers had gotten used to a huge and never-ending supply of cheap labor. In time the Depression lifted, the dust storms stopped, and the Hoovervilles vanished, but farming would never be the same again. Machines, migrants, and land consolidation had made it more a business than a way of life, and in that business the migrant worker would play an increasingly important part.

# HANDS
# FROM
# MEXICO

In December 1941, the United States officially entered World War II. The displaced sharecroppers and tenant farmers who had crowded migrant camps during the Depression now marched off to war or found lucrative jobs in war-related industries, leaving the big growers to face critical shortages of migrant farm labor. Out of this wartime emergency came the *bracero* program, which brought Mexican nationals across the border to work on American farms.

## THE PERFECT MIGRANTS

When the program began in 1942, it was supposed to be a temporary solution to a temporary problem. It lasted, in one form or another, until 1964, growing into a near-permanent institution because Mexican nationals provided American agribusiness with a seemingly inexhaustible pool of cheap, seasonal labor.

They came across the border when they were needed and went back home when the work was done. Domestic migrants (U.S. citizens in the seasonal labor force) waited out the off-seasons in Hispanic ghettoes called *colonias* or *barrios*. Many lived and traveled in family groups, creating a burden on medical, educational, and housing facilities.

The Mexicans left their families behind. The typical bracero was an adult male who lived in the roughest barracks without complaint and had little to distract him from his work. Historian Ernesto Galarza calls the braceros "folks with plenty of nothing."[1] They were poor, often illiterate farm workers who came from an authoritarian society of haciendas and land barons, where a lowly *peon* (peasant) owned no land, asked no questions, made no demands.

According to the U.S. Department of Agriculture, braceros accounted for about 93 percent of the temporary foreign work force employed on American farms from 1942 to 1964.[2] Other programs brought workers from the Bahamas, Canada, and the British West Indies. These workers were primarily employed along the East Coast of the United States. In the southwestern and Pacific Coast states, the bracero dominated the seasonal labor pool for more than twenty years. During that time, the program moved through three distinct phases—the first two operating by "gentleman's agreement" with the government of Mexico and the third created by an act of Congress that gave it the force and staying power of law.

## WORLD WAR II: 1942–45

In the summer of 1941, most of the world was already at war. Though the United States remained officially neutral, nobody expected that neutrality to last for long. Sooner or later, America would get into the fight, and the migrant labor pool would shrink as domestic farm workers traded their shovels and hoes for rifles and hand grenades. To prepare for these labor shortages, growers petitioned the government to bring in workers from Mexico for the 1941 harvest season. Although these early requests were rejected, it became clear that American agriculture would look south of the border for a solution to wartime manpower needs.

The United States formally entered the war in December 1941, and by spring of 1942 those expected shortages were a fact of life. The government began negotiations to bring Mexicans across the border for seasonal work on American farms. These first talks proved to be somewhat awkward; the Americans had a plan that they considered beneficial for both countries, but the Mexicans had a grudge. They had not forgotten the Depression years, when U.S. Immigration had expelled over fifty thousand Mexican nationals. The proud Mexicans regarded that action as an open insult, and so they were suspicious and distrustful of American intentions. In spite of this barrier, the two governments developed an agreement that was signed on July 23, 1942, and ratified by an exchange of diplomatic notes on August 4.

The first bracero program was enacted under authority of the Immigration Act of 1917. It placed the burden for recruiting, transporting, and repatriating Mexican nationals squarely on the shoulders of the U.S. government.

In 1942, Congress passed the Emergency Labor Supply Program, which included the bracero agreements in a more general plan for recruiting foreign workers to ease the manpower shortage on American farms. An amendment to the agreement with Mexico brought the bracero program into compliance with Article 29 of the Mexican labor law. This set forth detailed provisions regarding minimum wages, housing, and medical services for migrant farm workers from Mexico. Other amendments followed, each an informal diplomatic agreement tacked onto the original to further safeguard the interests of the braceros and bring the program into closer compliance with existing U.S. or Mexican laws. While these refinements were going on, administrative control of the program passed from the Farm Security Administration to

*With the United States' entry into World War II, many Mexican workers were offered jobs north of the border to fill the manpower shortage on American farms. These laborers came to be known as* braceros.

the newly created War Manpower Commission. This seemed to underline the temporary nature of the bracero program and gave Mexico an important role in the war effort. Instead of sending soldiers to the front, Mexico sent workers to the fields, and officials on both sides of the border recognized the importance of this contribution.

41

In 1944, Mexican foreign secretary Ezequiel Padilla spoke about the bracero agreements in glowing words: "They provide an opportunity to earn high wages, a noble adventure for our youth and above all, proof of our cooperation in the victory of our cause."[3]

In May 1945, Germany surrendered to Allied forces in Europe, and three months later, Japan followed suit in the Pacific. The State Department allowed a short interval to pass in order for the United States to stand down from the rigors of wartime preparedness, then on November 15, 1946, notified the Mexican government that the United States wished to terminate the bracero program.

Both Mexican farm workers and American farm owners greeted the news with dread. The Mexicans wanted the wages that only U.S. growers could pay, and the growers wanted the dependable source of migrant labor that had carried them through the war. American farmers predicted widespread economic chaos if the bracero program ended. They claimed that there was still a shortage of workers in the fields, still a need for braceros to supplement a shrinking force of domestic migrants. When the government yielded to this pressure and granted an extension, the bracero program entered its second stage.

## POSTWAR PROGRAMS: 1948–50

In January 1948, the War Manpower Commission was dissolved, and administration of the extended bracero agreements passed to the U.S. Department of Labor. Responsibility for recruiting and transporting the Mexican workers passed from the government to the employers themselves. The Mexican government worked through a bureau of migrant labor in their Department of Foreign Affairs. These widespread administrative changes gave rise to a great deal of confusion about exactly who was responsible for what phase of an increasingly complicated program.

In October 1948, controversy erupted on the Texas-Mexico border. The Texas cotton growers had set the prevailing wage for the first picking at $2.50 per hundred pounds—a wage that was promptly accepted by the local representative of the U.S. Department of Labor. Without advance warning or explanation, the Mexican government turned down the $2.50 rate and insisted that the wage be set at $3.00 per hundred pounds. The Department of Labor representatives were stunned, the growers outraged, and the would-be braceros desperate to work at any wage.

When the Mexican government threatened to close the border rather than allow the braceros to work at the $2.50 rate, some six thousand Mexican farm workers crossed the Rio Grande in a massive break. These men were arrested by the U.S. Border Patrol and then released in the custody of growers who wished to hire them. Charges and countercharges flew back and forth between the two governments. Mexico's secretary of foreign affairs, Jaime Torres Bodet, officially terminated the bracero agreements of 1948, and thousands of Mexican workers faced immediate recall from their American jobs. Eventually, the dispute was resolved with another diplomatic agreement, but the border incident of 1948 was only the beginning of a seemingly unstoppable tide of illegal immigration. For the first time since the beginning of the program, American farmers and Mexican workers feared disruption of a system that benefited both groups. To keep this from happening the workers took matters into their own hands.

## BRACEROS AND ILLEGALS: 1951–54

When Public Law 78 was enacted in 1951, it completely changed the character of the bracero agreements. Proponents saw it as a means of offering a lawful alternative to the increasingly troublesome traffic of illegals from

Mexico while also protecting American farmers from labor shortages caused by U.S. involvement in the Korean War. In theory, this latest of the bracero programs was still tied to emergency conditions in the farm labor market. In practice, Public Law 78 was an ongoing program with no clear end in sight. Foreign workers were becoming an integral part of the American migrant labor force. After Public Law 78 was passed, Congress enacted the Immigration and Nationality Act of 1952 (often referred to as the McCarren-Walter Act). Clause H-2 of this law established a permanent, ongoing program for employing foreign agricultural workers on American farms.

According to writer Victor J. Oliveira, the H-2 requirements were so strict that

> *the number of such workers admitted into the United States under the program was significantly less than that admitted under the Bracero and other programs. . . . (H-2) workers were primarily employed on the east coast because agricultural employers in the western United States had a readily available supply of illegal workers and therefore were less inclined to go through the legal procedures for participating in the H-2 program.*[4]

Southwestern agricultural employers found it to their advantage to use both legal and illegal workers from Mexico. According to U.S. Department of Agriculture figures, the number of legally admitted workers under Public Law 78 grew from 204,000 in 1951 to 321,000 in 1954, and even that did not eliminate the flood tide of illegals. The press called them wetbacks because so many came across the Rio Grande, drawn by higher wages and more jobs. In 1954, the Department of Immigration reported 1,108,900 illegals, and few officials would have been willing to guess how many more escaped detection by losing themselves in the migrant stream. Willard F. Kelley, assistant commissioner of the border patrol, called this "the greatest peacetime invasion complacently suffered by a country under open, flagrant, contemptuous violation of its law."[5] His words summarized the feelings of many U.S. officials, who saw the problem of illegal immigration slipping beyond their control. Despite protests from government and growing discontent from domestic migrant workers, southwestern farmers continued to hire both illegals and braceros to work in their fields. According to historian Ernesto Galarza, "the labor policy of commercial farmers and their associations consisted, on the one hand, of keeping the *bracero* machinery in working order . . . and on the other, of maintaining a substantial demand for Wetbacks as a counterweight." Galarza cited the example of the 1951 tomato harvest in California, which "was picked in about equal parts by *braceros* and illegals, with domestic workers, mostly in family groups, a poor third."[6] From the growers' standpoint, each group had its advantages and disadvantages.

Domestic family groups were legal but difficult to house; braceros were also legal but difficult to hire. Under Public Law 78, U.S. employers had to first make reasonable efforts to recruit domestic workers, then apply for government certification allowing them to hire a certain number of Mexicans for a specified period of time. It was always possible, though unlikely, that the government would refuse to give that certification.

Hiring illegals was a good deal simpler, largely because of the emergence of Spanish-speaking labor contractors, independent entrepreneurs who would hire whole crews of men, smuggle them across the border from Mexico, and even supervise them in the fields. Without contractors, the practice of hiring illegals could not have spread so readily through the whole of southwestern agriculture.

By 1954 it had become increasingly obvious that American immigration authorities could not enforce the laws against undocumented Mexican farm workers. On January 15, 1954, a joint press release from the Departments of State, Justice, and Labor announced a startling solution to the problem: eliminate illegal immigration by opening the border to all comers. Any Mexican could become a duly certified bracero simply by signing up at an office of the U.S. Immigration Service. In the first three days of the open-border program, 3,500 men crossed the border to sign up for work in American migrant crews. In Calexico, growers and labor contractors delivered illegals by the busload, transporting them to offices where a stroke of the pen changed them from "wetbacks" to braceros.

From the viewpoint of American farmers, Mexican migrant workers, and U.S. Immigration authorities, "Operation Wetback" was an outstanding success. The difficulties it would create, especially for citizen farm workers, hadn't yet become apparent in those heady summer days of 1954, when the chronic farm labor problem seemed well on the way to a permanent solution.

*After World War II ended,*
*Public Law 78 was enacted*
*to provide ongoing*
*employment opportunities*
*for foreign nationals.*
*However, due to strict*
*requirements governing*
*the hiring of braceros, many*
*growers turned to illegals*
*to harvest their crops.*

A
NEW
FEELING
IN THE
LAND

While Public Law 78 shaped the farm labor picture in the Southwest, other forces operated along the eastern seaboard, where African-Americans dominated the migrant labor force. These workers had to cope not only with the harshness of migrant life but with racial segregation that had the force of law and long tradition behind it. In 1955, those long-standing customs began to change. On December 1 of that year, a black seamstress named Rosa Parks refused to give up her seat on the bus when a white driver ordered her to move. She was promptly arrested for breaking racial segregation laws. That one event triggered the Montgomery Bus Boycott, led by a young minister named Martin Luther King, Jr. From these modest beginnings, the civil rights movement spread nationwide as African-Americans claimed their right to equality under the law. These advances scarcely touched the lives of blacks who made their living as migrant farm workers.

All along the eastern seaboard, a large and shifting population of migrants started each season picking citrus fruit in Florida, then moved north with the crops to finish the harvest in Maine. For these people, voter registration drives, school desegregation projects, and equal opportunity employment programs had little meaning. They never stayed in one place long enough to have an address, let alone register to vote.

48

# MIGRANTS IN THE EASTERN STREAM

The end of World War II brought an exodus of blacks from the rural South to major urban centers, as men returning from war found they could not go back to farming. The changes that had begun during the Depression continued through the war years, as the mechanical cotton picker and other machines made farms bigger and more mechanized. These corporate farms of the South needed the same thing their western counterparts had needed since the turn of the century: a large and mobile force of migrant workers who would appear during peak seasons and vanish without a trace when the work was done. Growers worked through black crew leaders to ensure that the laborers would appear when needed, and through local police to ensure that they would leave when finished.

East Coast crew leaders worked in much the same way as West Coast labor contractors: recruiting and supervising large crews of migrant workers. When psychiatrist Robert Coles interviewed a number of these men, he found an intense love-hate bond between the crew leader and "his" workers.

"I do anything you can imagine for them," said one crew leader. "I wake them up in the morning, or else a lot of them would sleep on and on. . . . I take them to the field and get them started. Before that I make sure they've had some breakfast in them. I bring them food to prepare. I tell them when to sleep, and I make sure they [don't] fight."[1]

To the migrant, the crew leader was practically a god; a shrewd, resourceful person who knew his way around the white, landowning world. Migrants who worked on their own were vulnerable to harassment or arrest: "The police are always looking to see if we're not keeping moving," one young migrant told Robert Coles. "If they catch you sitting by the road, they'll take you to jail. . . . They'll tell you that if you're going to be picking, you've got to go ahead and pick, then you've got to get away, fast."[2]

Every migrant knew the unwritten rule: work or keep moving. A common practice was to round up unemployed migrants and give them a choice between working in the fields or doing time in jail. Those who agreed to work lived in tarpaper shacks, worked twelve to fourteen hours a day, and were often forced to buy their food and other necessities from the grower at inflated prices. In states with minimum-wage laws, farmers commonly evaded those laws by a system writer Peter Matthiessen describes as "downtime." "When a machine breaks down or a truck is delayed or when, for any reason, the employee is not actually working, he may be laid off during the workday, or not put on the payroll until noon."[3]

In the cities and towns of the South, African-Americans made slow but steady progress in their struggle for civil rights. On the dusty back roads, migrant farm workers kept right on moving from crop to ripened crop, scarcely aware of the changes going on around them.

## THE BRACERO LEGACY

There were two other main streams of migrant workers, one beginning in south Texas and heading northward through the Midwest, another going from southern California all the way up to the Canadian border. For these two groups Public Law 78 had its greatest effect. By the late fifties, this last of the bracero programs had made its impact on every facet of migrant life, from hiring practices to wages, housing, and working conditions.

Migrants in the field were exposed to many health hazards, from pesticide residues to lack of common amenities like drinking water and field toilets. Serious as these problems were, none created the emotional impact of *el cortito*, the short-handled hoe.

*El cortito* was an ordinary hoe with a handle only

slightly longer than that of a hand trowel. To use it, a worker couldn't stand up straight, nor could he kneel. He had to crouch, twisting his back into a torturous position for hours at a time.

According to writer George Horowitz, growers began using the short-handled hoe after World War II, when bracero labor still came cheap. " 'Only a Mexican would stoop so low for a dollar,' the growers said. 'Only a grower would stoop so low to save one,' the Mexicans answered. And so the dialogue began."[4]

Thinning with the short-handled hoe was one of the most dreaded jobs in the field. A worker would have to double over, working his way down mile-long rows without touching his knees to the ground or straightening up between plants. "I think," said union organizer Cesar Chavez, "this is where the employer shows the most contempt for his workers. . . . [Growers] look at human beings as implements. If they had any consideration for the torture that people go through, they would give up the short-handled hoe. All that stooping is one reason farm workers die before they're fifty."[5]

Long after Public Law 78 ended, el cortito remained a fact of migrant life and an ongoing source of disagreement between the growers who devised it and the workers who had to use it. Governor Edmund G. (Jerry) Brown, Jr., banned it from California fields early in 1975. Its use continued in Texas until 1981, when the state legislature passed a law against it, an action that migrant farm workers hailed as a milestone in their long struggle for better working conditions.

The impact of Public Law 78 wasn't limited to conditions in the fields. It affected every phase of migrant life, from wages and working conditions to medical care and housing. With braceros readily available, growers found it cheaper to maintain barracks for single men rather than cabins for family groups. Because domestic migrants (those who did not return to Mexico between seasons)

51

*With* el cortito, *a short-handled hoe, farm workers had to stay bent over for hours at a time. Its use was banned in California in 1975.*

often traveled and worked in family groups, they were forced to find lodging in nearby barrios, where the rents were so high that parents had to put their children to work just to make ends meet. A farm worker and union organizer named Roberto Acuna told writer Studs Terkel what it was like to grow up in a migrant family during those years when the bracero was king:

> *I started picking crops when I was eight. . . . We used to work early, about four o'clock in the morning. We'd pick the harvest until about six. Then we'd run home and get into our supposedly clean clothes and*

*run all the way to school because we'd be late. . . .
[After school] we'd rush home, change clothes, go
back to work until seven, seven-thirty in the evening.
On Saturday and Sunday, we'd be there from four-
thirty in the morning until about seven-thirty in the
evenings.*[6]

Migrant life was a great deal simpler for the Mexican
national. A careful bracero could pay for his food and
lodging and still take the bulk of his earnings back to
Mexico, where a lower cost of living made his American
wages seem like a small fortune. The most frugal domestic migrant could barely stretch his earnings beyond the
immediate needs of each harvest season. Growers were
well aware of these fundamental differences between braceros and domestics, and their dependence on a large
labor force from Mexico continued to grow.

By the end of the fifties, domestic workers had all but
disappeared from California's migrant labor force. If they
went to likely farms during harvest season they were apt
to see NO PICKERS WANTED signs posted at the gates,
while a full crew of braceros labored in the field. If
they applied at growers' association offices, interviewers
discouraged them from making the effort, citing difficult
paperwork, low wages, back-breaking work, and no family housing. As an example of the bracero dominance in
California fields, Ernesto Galarza cites the Ventura
County lemon harvest of 1960, which employed 2,500
braceros and only 150 domestics. That same season, the
tomato fields near San Jose employed 8,530 braceros and
860 domestics.[7]

## THE ACTION IN OXNARD

In August of 1958, a young man named Cesar Chavez
arrived in Oxnard, California, to establish an office of
the Community Service Organization (CSO). Chavez in-

53

*To make ends meet, many braceros have*
*their children join them in the fields.*

tended to start voter registration drives, citizenship classes, and other self-help projects in the Mexican-American community. He ended up spearheading a determined effort to secure farm jobs for domestic migrants who were being passed over in favor of braceros.

Chavez had a special interest in the plight of migrant farm workers. He was a former migrant himself, who began working the fields when he was ten years old. The action in Oxnard was to be a turning point in his life. When it began, he was a young and idealistic man with a vague desire to do something for farm workers. By the time it ended, he was a determined advocate who would soon become to western migrants what Martin Luther King, Jr., had become to southern blacks.

When Chavez arrived in Oxnard, he thought the biggest issue in the Mexican-American community would be a dangerous railroad crossing near the barrio. Over the years several had died there; Chavez himself had gone to school with one of the victims. "When I mentioned [the crossing] people weren't aroused," he told his biographer, Jacques Levy. "Instead, they began to come at me with the *bracero* issue. That was an issue that I didn't even expect."[8]

Cesar Chavez was not without sympathy for the men who left their homes in Mexico to work in American fields, but he was beginning to see larger issues in this situation, issues that affected both braceros and domestics. Americans dared not protest wages or working conditions for fear of losing their jobs to braceros, and braceros dared not complain for fear of being returned to Mexico.

At the beginning of the Oxnard project, Chavez made a study of exactly how the hiring system worked. For two weeks, he got up before dawn and presented himself at the Oxnard labor camp, dressed and ready for work. He needed a referral slip, they said, and sent him to the Farm

Placement Service in Ventura, eight miles away. By the time he got back to Oxnard with his referral, all of that day's jobs had been filled. When he returned the next morning and presented the same referral slip, the dispatcher said it was outdated and therefore useless. Chavez carefully documented every effort.

In time, he persuaded others to go with him. Up to a dozen migrant farm workers carpooled to Ventura, presented themselves at the Farm Placement Office, and patiently completed the forms that placement officials gave them. These forms were lengthy and complicated. Chavez filled them out for those who didn't know English well enough to do it themselves. The workers kept copies of everything, quietly building up a file to document the problems domestic migrants faced when they tried to get work. Armed with this evidence and led by Chavez, the Oxnard workers staged protest marches, public demonstrations, and field sit-ins to bring public attention to their plight. The techniques that had worked for Martin Luther King, Jr., in Montgomery, Alabama, now worked equally well for Cesar Chavez in Oxnard, California. Growers began calling the CSO office for whole crews of domestic workers rather than risk being exposed as violators of Public Law 78. The office became a clearinghouse, matching hundreds of North American migrants with available jobs.

Cesar Chavez saw the possibility of building a strong farm workers' union on the foundation of CSO's success in Oxnard. He had eighteen hundred workers, a functioning organization, and a group of growers who might be willing to negotiate meaningful labor contracts. All he needed was a go-ahead from CSO. That, he soon realized, would be a long time coming. The board of directors considered union activity beyond the scope of CSO's work, which was community self-help, not labor relations. Instead of funding Chavez's work in Oxnard, they

56

*Through careful study of working conditions in California, Cesar Chavez was able to organize both braceros and domestic farm workers to effectively demand better pay and fair labor practices.*

transferred him to the Los Angeles office. Within six months, the Oxnard structure had collapsed, and the braceros were back in force.

Though the Oxnard action did not result in long-lasting improvements for migrant farm workers, it did show Cesar Chavez what might be accomplished by hard work, dedication, and group solidarity. His desire to "do something for farm workers" was no longer a fuzzy, unfocused dream. He had decided exactly what he wanted to do: organize a union.

CSO still wasn't interested in the project. Some board members thought any effort to organize farm workers would be doomed to failure as long as growers had access to a plentiful supply of braceros. Others simply thought that union organizing should be the job of big-time labor groups like the AFL-CIO. For two years, Chavez pushed his idea of organizing a union for migrant farm workers. He thought he'd almost won the day when Saul Alinsky, head of the foundation that funded CSO, came out in favor of the plan. In March 1962 at the CSO convention in Calexico, Chavez had high hopes of seeing his dream become a reality. Instead, he saw it voted down by the membership. Chavez promptly stood in front of that assembly and said two words: "I resign." He went back to his Los Angeles office to clean up loose ends.

Two weeks later, on March 31, 1962, he left CSO behind him. It was his thirty-fifth birthday, a fact that was not lost on friends, coworkers, and newspaper reporters. "I've heard people say," Chavez told his biographer, "that because I was thirty-five, I was getting worried, as I hadn't done too much in my life. . . . I didn't care about that. I just knew we needed a union."[9] Chavez set to work to answer that need. He made speeches at rallies, gave talks at smaller house meetings, and slowly recruited a core group. When he felt he had enough support, he called an organizing convention.

On September 30, 1962, at an abandoned theater in Fresno, California, the National Farm Workers Association was born. It was part of the events that would turn the sixties into a decade of social upheaval. On the other side of the country, a young African-American named James Meredith gained admission to the previously all-white University of Mississippi, southern blacks registered to vote in unprecedented numbers, and Martin Luther King, Jr., continued to preach his message of racial integration and equality under the law. The time was ripe for change, and migrant farm workers began to believe that they could be part of this widespread struggle for a better life.

# THE
# FOUNDING
# OF A
# UNION

On May 29, 1963, the House of Representatives voted to terminate Public Law 78, thus ending the last bracero program, more than twenty years after the first one began. Growers warned of crops rotting in the field while food prices soared, of bankruptcies and layoffs in the United States, and total economic collapse in Mexico. According to Ernesto Galarza, their real fear was not of massive manpower shortages but of domestic migrants ''who were discovering the possibilities of community life, experimenting with economic organization and talking of collective bargaining. Emerging slowly out of the flux of the labor pool these were the first footings of a countervailing force that might some day face the [growers'] associations on even terms.''[1]

By the time Public Law 78 ended, Cesar Chavez and a dedicated group of volunteers had been organizing the National Farm Workers Association for nearly eight months. The union was still weak and underfinanced, but it was in the right place at the right time to become a focal point for postbracero migrants in the western stream. All over the country, 1963 was a year of changes. The civil rights movement that began with the Montgomery bus boycott of the fifties crescendoed in August 1963, when two hundred thousand people marched on Washington

D.C., to demonstrate for civil rights and listen to Martin Luther King's famous "I Have a Dream" speech.

Cesar Chavez also had a dream; he wanted a better life for migrant farm workers, and to him the best way to achieve that goal was by forming a union that would be strong enough to take on the forces of big-time agribusiness. It was not going to be an easy task; from the very beginning, Chavez expected an uphill fight.

## SPREADING THE WORD

In the earliest days of NFWA, Public Law 78 was alive and healthy, with no end to it yet in sight. Chavez had no financing, no major labor organization in his corner. Massive rallies were out of the question. There was no money for such things. Chavez knew he would have to start slowly and feel his way into the task. He chose the town of Delano, which seemed uniquely suited to become a starting point for the new union.

There were more than thirty-eight thousand acres of grape vineyards around the town, and grapes require constant tending through nine months of the year. The farm workers of Delano were therefore less migratory than most; some even lived there year-round. The relative stability of the farm worker population would simplify the task of organizing.

Having selected a place to start, Chavez began his work in the most direct way he could imagine—by driving from farm to farm, talking with workers in the fields. When he asked what they thought about starting a union, some said it sounded okay, some called it foolish, and some turned away without saying a word. Nobody wanted to open up to a stranger who showed up out of nowhere, asking questions about something as revolutionary as a union for migrant farm workers.

To meet with people in a friendlier environment, Chavez fell back on the CSO technique of small, informal house meetings. He held the first on May 31, 1962, just two months after he walked out of the CSO convention to start a union. At their own homes, surrounded by family and friends, people talked more freely. Most of them thought a union would be a wonderful idea, but they also thought it couldn't be done. The growers were just too powerful, the braceros too easily available, the workers themselves too rootless to form meaningful associations. Chavez didn't press. He knew as well as anyone that migrant farm workers on the West Coast had seen unions come and seen them go. From the 1913 riots in Wheatland to the 1928 melon strikes in the Imperial Valley and the 1936 lettuce strike in Salinas, "union" meant strikes and strikes meant trouble.

Instead of labor unions, Chavez talked about "associations," "cooperatives," and "self-help groups." Instead of speeches and lectures about the benefits of such groups, he demonstrated those benefits by helping people with their problems. If a migrant family needed a place to live, he helped them find it. If they needed a dependable car or medical care or someone who knew the ins and outs of dealing with social service agencies, Cesar Chavez stood ready to give them the help they needed.

Reverend James Drake of the Migrant Ministry was one of the first to believe in Cesar Chavez and his dream. "Building the union was a slow, plodding thing based on hard work and very personal relationships," he told Chavez biographer Jacques Levy.

*Workers were not organized in dramatic meetings, but one by one, in a car on the way to a labor commissioner hearing, or while driving to meet an industrial accident referee. And while the new member drove, Chavez talked. He talked clearly and carefully, and*

*the plan was set forth . . . a growing number of farm*
*workers passed the word, "If you have trouble, go to*
*Delano. Chavez can help."*[2]

In this slow and painstaking way, the membership grew, and so did the staff of organizers. Chavez got his whole family involved in the work and also brought in former CSO colleagues, such as the fiery young activist Dolores Huerta, who would stay to become vice president of the union and one of its most courageous proponents. By the time Chavez called the first organizing convention the NFWA had over two hundred dues-paying members.

Chavez was well aware that this first gathering would be the beginning of a new, public phase in the development of NFWA. Now the goal would be to build organizational structure, solidarity, and pride. For that, NFWA needed a constitution and bylaws; it needed stirring songs, mottoes, and rallying cries that would bind migrant farm workers together and represent their aspirations to the outside world. In the months before the Fresno convention, Cesar Chavez and his staff set to work, constructing a foundation for NFWA.

## UNDER THE BLACK EAGLE

Everyone on the organizing committee agreed that the new union needed a flag of its very own. That flag should be vivid and dramatic, without looking like the work of a professional designer. It should be a homegrown flag, a flag that anyone could make and everyone could love. Chavez chose the colors—red, white, and black. His brother Richard drew a stylized eagle and his cousin Manuel volunteered to make the first flag.

The organizing committee planned to unveil the new flag at the Fresno convention. For maximum dramatic effect, they kept it covered until the delegates were all assembled and the time seemed right. Then Manuel Chavez pulled a cord, the paper covering fell away, and a startled murmur rippled through the crowd. Some members worried that the new flag looked ''sort of communist,'' while others thought it was too much like the hated red, white, and black swastika flag of Nazi Germany.

The banner that was supposed to be the symbol of unity became an object of discord, as those who liked the black eagle argued with those who didn't like it at all. It was Manuel Chavez who finally saved the day, leaping to his feet and shouting to be heard over all the turmoil: ''When that damn eagle flies, the problems of the farm workers will be solved!''

The audience broke into applause, and the black eagle became the official symbol of their union. By the time the Fresno convention ended, the delegates had also voted to elect temporary officers, lobby for a minimum-wage law covering farm workers, and charge dues of $3.50 per month. They adopted a motto to go with the flag: Viva la causa!—Long live the cause!

## THE CONSTITUTIONAL CONVENTION

Drafting a workable constitution for the new union turned out to be a long, difficult process. Before putting a word on paper, Chavez assembled copies of as many union constitutions as he could find. For days he studied them, trying to understand the strengths and weaknesses of each. In all those hours of reading, one thing became clear: structures that worked for industrial unions would not necessarily work for NFWA. More than one effort to unionize farm workers had failed because it had used methods better suited to industrial workers who led stable, settled lives.

Cesar Chavez set out to draw up a constitution for unsettled workers—migrants, whose only real home was

*Cesar Chavez at a rally in New York in 1971.*
*The UFW flag in the background was criticized*
*at first for its similarity to the flag of Nazi Germany,*
*but was eventually chosen to represent the union.*

the road they traveled. The challenge was to make the union flexible enough to meet their needs anywhere they happened to be yet stable enough to become a fixed point of reference in otherwise rootless lives.

"I thought," Chavez told Jacques Levy, "that we would need a very strong, centralized administration, and that we could never have a local as other unions have.

We couldn't have any geographical restrictions on employment, and I felt that the Union would have to be so alike everywhere that workers could recognize that it was, in fact, one union."[3]

A preliminary draft of the constitution was presented at Fresno in 1962; then on January 21, 1963, the final version was accepted at a constitutional convention in Delano. The preamble to that constitution made a clear statement of reality as migrant farm workers had come to view it:

> *We the Farm Workers of America, have tilled the soil, sown the seeds and harvested the crops. We have provided food in abundance for the people in the cities, and the nation and the world but have not had sufficient food to feed our own children.*
>
> *While industrial workers, living and working in one place, have joined together and grown strong, we have been isolated, scattered and hindered from uniting our forces.*[4]

At the Delano convention, the constitution was presented and approved, permanent officers were elected, and the union that began as one man's dream became a full-fledged reality, complete with flag, motto, constitution, and duly elected officers. In spite of these trappings of organization, NFWA was still on shaky ground, and no one knew that better than Cesar Chavez. Public Law 78 was still in effect when the union drafted its constitution. The memberhsip was small and the resources few. Even the most optimistic organizers didn't believe that NFWA would have a chance of winning a major strike.

Chavez agreed with them. To make NFWA succeed where others had failed, he planned to build a solid, financially stable base before calling any kind of strike. This position reassured the workers, most of whom feared the very idea of taking any action that their employers might regard as hostile. For more than two years, Chavez and his volunteer staff kept busy helping members, lobbying state legislators, and building their organization.

By spring of 1965, Public Law 78 was no longer a threat, and NFWA embarked on its first small-scale, localized strikes. To maximize their chances of success, Chavez and his staff targeted specific, well-documented problems: a wage dispute among rose grafters in McFarland and a rent increase at a labor camp in Tulare.

The rose strike began when NFWA learned that rose grafters who had been promised $9 per thousand plants were actually earning between $6.50 and $7 per thousand. The work these people did was highly skilled; cutting tiny, perfectly placed slits in mature rosebushes and inserting live buds. One slip of the knife, one bad placement of a graft could ruin an entire plant.

In the interest of simplicity, the union targeted only one company, the largest in McFarland, which employed more than eighty-five grafters. The strike was scheduled to begin on a Monday morning at the height of the grafting season. In the predawn hours, NFWA officers drove around to the workers' homes, making sure that everyone honored the strike. Though a few may have wavered at the beginning, not a single rose grafter showed up for work that day. The company foreman was so angry that he refused to talk with anyone from the union. Dolores Huerta, who was by then vice president of NFWA, went to the company's offices, only to be confronted by policemen who ordered her to leave or face arrest.

The McFarland rose strike was over in a matter of days, broken by labor contractors who defied the workers with hastily recruited crews of inexperienced people who would do what they were told to do and take the wages they were offered. Though NFWA didn't win the McFarland strike, they still made some modest gains. The growers never met with anyone from NFWA, never recognized the grafters' right to collective bargaining, and never admitted that they had been unfair in the way they set wages. They did, however, give the grafters a temporary wage increase that lasted until the end of that year's grafting season. The experience also gave NFWA a firsthand look at the kind of tactics striking farm workers could expect to face in the future.

At about the same time as the McFarland rose strike, the Tulare County Housing Authority decided to raise rents in its migrant labor camps. The agency proposed to charge twenty-five dollars a month for tin shacks with no running water. Reverend Jim Drake of the Migrant Ministry joined with former CSO worker Gilbert Padilla to organize a rent strike that lasted most of the summer. NFWA came to help, and the strike these groups mounted became an inspiring success story; the tin shacks, which had been considered temporary even during the Depression, were torn down and replaced by modest but livable cottages.

Years later, recalling the incident for his biographer, Cesar Chavez still remembered the Tulare County rent strike as one of the first times the black eagle flew. In terms the workers could understand, the strike served to demonstrate that the union was a functioning organization concerned with their problems. The officers of NFWA felt good about what they accomplished in the summer of 1965. It wasn't a time of earthshaking victories, but it was a promising beginning to a struggle that would prove to be both difficult and lengthy.

# VIVA
# LA CAUSA!
# STRIKES
# AND
# BOYCOTTS

The late sixties was a time of activism on many different fronts. African-Americans continued to demonstrate for civil rights, college students demonstrated for free speech, and people from all walks of life demonstrated against American involvement in Vietnam. Migrant farm workers joined the spirit of the times, pressing their own case for better wages and working conditions through the use of strikes, boycotts, marches, and rallies.

## THE GREAT GRAPE STRIKE

NFWA's first major strike happened almost by accident, before Cesar Chavez and his staff felt they were ready for such a large-scale effort. On September 8, 1965, Filipino grape workers, led by Larry Itliong of the Agricultural Workers Organizing Committee (AWOC), called a strike against the grape growers of Delano. Ready or not, Chavez felt that NFWA was morally obligated to support the Filipinos. He sat down with his staff and decided to call an emergency meeting of the membership to ask for a strike vote. Chavez scheduled the meeting for September 16, Mexican Independence Day, hoping that the spirit of the holiday would create a groundswell of support for the strike. There was a general mood of excitement as the workers assembled at Our Lady of

Guadalupe Church in Delano. "By the time the meeting started," Chavez told Jacques Levy, "the hall and balcony were jam-packed. . . . There were guys from every ranch in the area. We made sure of that so, when a strike vote was taken, it would be a general strike of all growers. The meeting was very spirited, a band played, and every so often the hall rang out with cries of 'Viva la causa!' "[1] Riding on a tide of emotion, the membership voted to support the AWOC strike. On the following Monday, more than twelve hundred members failed to report for work.

As in the McFarland rose strike, the growers refused to negotiate with the union or even to recognize it as a bargaining agent for the workers. Unlicensed labor contractors brought in crews of "scabs" (strikebreakers), and local authorities restricted picketing at the fields where the strikebreakers were working. With the strike broken and pickets banned, NFWA turned to the boycott, which was to become one of its most powerful weapons. The first boycotts were loosely organized efforts, with crews of picketers assigned to follow the scab grapes wherever they went. The idea was to make certain that everyone knew these grapes had been picked by strikebreakers. At first union members tried to follow all the grapes, but it soon became clear that they were spreading their forces too thin. In December they decided to concentrate their efforts on Schenley Wines. Volunteers went to cities all over the country, asking people not to purchase Schenley products.

By spring of 1966, strike-and-boycott had become a way of life for the union members; the officers of NFWA and AWOC planned strategies and raised money for the strike fund, rank-and-file members walked picket lines, and still the growers refused to talk. Cesar Chavez began looking for another grand gesture to focus public attention on the plight of migrant farm workers. The idea of a long, well-publicized march took shape slowly, formed from the ideas of several different people. For inspiration the organizers had the long Mexican tradition of religious pilgrimages and the more recent example of Dr. Martin Luther King, Jr., and his march on Washington.

There was a great deal of discussion about where the march ought to go: whether to Mexico, protesting the crews of strikebreakers that came across the border under U.S. Immigration's new "green card" rules, to Schenley's West Coast offices in San Francisco, or even all the way to New York, home of Schenley's national headquarters. The discussion lasted until NFWA learned that the Fair Trade Act passed by the California state legislature set a minimum price for liquor, thus protecting Schenley's income, while farm workers were denied a minimum wage for their labors.

Everyone agreed that the state capitol building in Sacramento should be their destination. Chavez timed the march carefully so that it would come to a grand climax in Sacramento on Easter Sunday morning. The planning staff set up three teams to share responsibility for the project. One team went ahead to organize food and housing along the way, a second stayed with the marchers to handle arrangements at each stopover, and a third stayed behind to organize migrant workers in places where the union was not yet active. All along the way, people turned out to wish the pilgrims well. In Modesto, Bill Kircher, national director of organizing for AFL-CIO, arranged a demonstration of support by local members of the huge labor organization. In Stockton, the Anglo mayor joined with leaders of the Mexican-American community to put on a fiesta honoring the marchers. In Sacramento, ten thousand people turned out to greet them when they arrived on Easter Sunday.

The success of the march drew nationwide attention to the plight of California farm workers and strengthened the boycott of Schenley Wines. Before the march ended, Schenley finally agreed to open negotiations with NFWA, and by June, the union had its first major contract. The agreement with Schenley recognized NFWA as the bargaining agent for the farm workers, set a wage of $1.75 an hour, and established a union hiring hall where migrant workers could apply for available jobs without having to go through a labor contractor.

In the aftermath of victory, NFWA and AWOC agreed to make their temporary alliance a permanent one. In August 1966 the two groups merged and took a new name: United Farm Workers Organizing Committee (UF-WOC). As other wineries followed Schenley to the bargaining table, the new union turned its attention to growers of table grapes. In 1967, Chavez and his staff launched a nationwide boycott of table grapes. That boycott lasted until 1970, touching the lives of growers, retailers, and consumers as well as farm workers. According to Coachella Valley grower Lionel Steinberg, "This social, political boycott effort, which is unparalleled in American history, literally closed Boston, New York, Philadelphia, Chicago, Detroit, Montreal, Toronto completely from handling table grapes. It took several years for the boycott to be that effective. It just gradually closed in like a noose around the necks of the vineyardists."[2]

The nationwide impact of the boycott not only strengthened UFWOC's negotiating position in California but inspired farm workers in other parts of the country to band together and try to improve their own wages and working conditions.

## THE TEXAS MELON STRIKE

During the Schenley boycott, a union volunteer named Eugene Nelson set out from California to organize boycott efforts in Chicago. Along the way he stopped in Texas to visit a friend and ended up staying to begin a strike in the melon fields of Starr County.

Migrant farm workers in south Texas sometimes earned as little as forty cents an hour. They were poorly fed, badly housed, and greatly in need of an organization strong enough to stand up for their rights. When the California union signed that first, historic contract with Schenley Wines, a tremor of excitement ran through the labor camps and barrios of south Texas. The time was right, the workers hopeful, and so Eugene Nelson decided to stay and see what he could do.

On May 22, 1966, Nelson kicked off an organizing drive with a rally in Rio Grande City. A week later, the Independent Workers' Association (IWA) had seven hundred members and was preparing to strike eight major growers in Starr County. The growers eventually broke that strike but not before word had spread of the farm workers' plight all over the state of Texas.

According to Juanita Valdez-Cox, in an unpublished history of the Starr County strike, the largest and most memorable event of the entire action was a march from San Juan to the state capitol in Austin, five hundred miles away. As a veteran of the march on Sacramento, Eugene Nelson knew well the power of pilgrimages; they brought people together, attracted media attention, and aroused widespread public interest. Taking a page from UF-WOC's book, Nelson timed the Texas march to end on a major holiday—in this case, Labor Day. Though the pilgrimage made a dramatic demonstration it fell short of its underlying goal.

Juanita Valdez-Cox wrote,

*From the very beginning, the goal of the march had been to bring pressure on Governor Connally to call a special session of the Legislature for the purpose of*

73

Though denied the chance to see the governor in Austin, the marchers kept going, arriving as planned on the steps of the capitol building, where they were greeted by cheering crowds of well-wishers.

As the melon strike moved into its second year, Governor Connally sent a troop of Texas Rangers into Starr County with instructions to control the protesters. Stories began coming out of south Texas, telling of pickets being subject to mass arrest, harassment, and even beatings. In the summer of 1967, Cesar Chavez went into Starr County to see if he could calm a situation that was ripe for violence. The hard-pressed farm workers were ready to do anything, even fight, to get rid of the Rangers. Chavez sympathized with their goal but could not condone the use of violence to achieve it. He asked for a chance to seek a peaceful solution, and the workers of Starr County agreed.

Chavez set to work right away. With the help of IWA member Magdaleon Dimas, he organized a prayer vigil. A group of women, all dressed in black, assembled on the steps of the hotel where the Rangers were staying. There they stood, quietly praying for the souls of the Texas Rangers, who could only watch in stunned silence. Twenty-four hours later, Governor Connally pulled the special troop out of town.

74

*In the midst of the violent Texas melon strike in 1966, a peaceful march from Starr County to Austin attracted media attention to the struggle of farm workers.*

On July 12, 1967, U.S. Secretary of Labor Willard Wirtz declared six Starr County farms strikebound, thus making it illegal for those farmers to replace striking domestic workers with ''green card'' crews from Mexico. The action, according to Juanita Valdez-Cox, was too little, too late: the melon harvest was nearly over, the workers already heading north to pick crops throughout the Midwest. By the time those workers returned to south Texas, the strike was dead.

Though the Starr County strike did not result in union contracts, higher wages, or better working conditions, it did have an impact. Events such as the Austin march and the prayer vigil sensitized the public to the plight of migrant farm workers in Texas and laid a foundation for future efforts to improve their working and living conditions.

## ORGANIZING OHIO

In 1967, a twenty-year-old college student named Baldemar Velasquez launched the Farm Labor Organizing Committee (FLOC) in Toledo, Ohio, with a press conference, a small bilingual newspaper, and a handful of charter members. As the third of nine children in a family of migrant farm workers, Velasquez knew the people and the way they lived. As a sociology student at Bluffton College, he knew the social activism that launched the civil rights movement in the South and the farm worker unions in California and Texas.

Like others who had tried to organize migrants, Velasquez realized that the union would have to be flexible enough to accommodate a membership that was constantly on the move and yet be stable enough to bring a sense of permanence into the workers' fragmented lives. He did not plan to begin his work with strikes, protests, and elaborate contract negotiations. He wanted to educate migrant workers about their rights, recruit members, and build a strong foundation for a union that would someday become a respected voice for migrant farm workers all over the Midwest.

He started out by getting himself arrested for entering the Libby-McNeil-Libby plant in Leipsic, Ohio, to distribute the FLOC newspaper. "We used the opportunity to try to force a legal decision on whether we can go into migrant camps to try to work with the workers,'' Velasquez told the *Bluffton News* in a story published September 21, 1967. ''Several growers and employers have refused to let us come into the camps to distribute the newspapers or talk to the workers. But this is treating the workers like prisoners. They rent the camp housing from the companies and growers; they shouldn't be told who they can hear or what they can read.''

When Velasquez went to the Libby plant, he brought a Catholic priest, several FLOC members, and an entire sociology class from Bluffton College that was doing a field study on social movements. These people did not attempt to accompany Velasquez into the Libby plant. They waited at the door to offer their moral support and to witness his arrest.

The practice of bringing along witnesses paid off later, when attorney Jack Gannon and a group of FLOC members accompanied Velasquez to a farm in Putnam County. When they tried to talk to the workers, the farmer drove his pickup truck straight into Velasquez and later took a punch at Jack Gannon. FLOC got a tape recording of the farmer admitting that he deliberately drove into Velasquez and a photograph of him trying to hit Gannon. With this evidence, the union pressed charges against the farmer.

In reaction to this incident, other Putnam County growers banded together and reached an agreement with FLOC, allowing the union to enter the camps and talk with workers. In signing this agreement, the growers of Putnam County, Ohio made history: it was the first time an association of farm owners made any kind of agreement with a union of farm workers. To Baldemar Velasquez and his organizers, the Putnam County accords not only opened labor camps to their message but opened lines of communication with the growers who owned those camps.

Building on this initial success, FLOC moved into Lucas County, where they tried to organize a meeting between farmers and workers. When that effort failed to establish wide-scale dialogue, FLOC decided to concentrate on one grower at a time, beginning with the John Ackerman farm. Their approach was simple and direct: offer Ackerman an alternative between signing a contract or being faced with a strike. When repeated efforts failed to get a meeting, the cry of *"Huelga!"* (strike) ran through the ranks. Picketing began on a Friday evening. By Sunday, Ackerman and several other growers had agreed to meet with FLOC. By Monday night, the union had signed twenty-one contracts that recognized FLOC as bargaining agent for the workers and set certain standards for wages, benefits, and working conditions. Those contracts were a major concession for the growers and a resounding victory for the workers.

As the sixties came to a close, the problems of migrant farm workers still weren't solved, but for the first time ever, they were out in the open. The public was sensitized to farm worker issues, and migrants themselves had a new sense of pride in their work and hope for their future.

# TAKING
# THE
# LONG
# VIEW

By the 1970s farm worker unions had become a fact of life in rural America. Though resistance from agribusiness, government, and even organized labor often defeated their efforts, the unions did succeed in bringing the problems of migrant workers to the attention of writers seeking material, activists seeking a cause, and scientists studying the effects of poverty and rootlessness on the individual, the family, and the community.

## FOCUS ON MIGRANT FARM WORKERS

At one time or another in the late sixties and early seventies, each of the three migrant streams (eastern, midwestern, western) received its share of attention. Close scrutiny revealed that each area had problems unique to its particular environment along with a host of difficulties common to all. Studies from all parts of the country added up to a grim picture of migrant life.

The *Congressional Record* for October 11, 1968, included a UFWOC report on conditions in the western stream:

>    *Infant mortality: 125% higher than the national rate.*
>    *Maternal mortality: 125% higher than the national rate.*

*Influenza and pneumonia: 200% higher than the national rate.*

*Tuberculosis and other infectious diseases: 260% higher than the national rate.*

*Accidents: 300% higher than the national rate.*

*Life expectancy for migrants is 49 years, as opposed to 70 for all others.*[1]

Other studies in other places have indicated that these figures would apply equally well in the East and Midwest.

Television journalist Edward R. Murrow brought eastern-stream migrants to public attention with *Harvest of Shame*, a 1960 documentary exploring conditions in the sugarcane fields and migrant labor camps of Florida. Three years later, psychiatrist Robert Coles published an account of his research with eastern migrants. He wrote at length about the skills migrants had to develop simply to make it from day to day.

*Migrant farmers . . . are essentially the rural poor who have shunned becoming the urban unemployed. They are people who know a great deal about how to survive on little money. . . . They know how to buy stale bread at low cost, or soda pop instead of milk for their children. They know that candy takes you a long way on its calories and that, for a pittance, fat, which subdues hunger, can be obtained.*[2]

Writer Vance Packard used migrant farm workers as an extreme example of the rootlessness that he saw developing in all segments of American society. In his 1972 book, *A Nation of Strangers*, he noted that the middle-stream migrants of south Texas went to great lengths to preserve a sense of community. During harvest season they traveled in stable crews made up of relatives and long-term friends who had worked together for years. In

80

winter they returned to the Rio Grande Valley, where many families owned or were buying their homes.

According to the Texas Conference of Churches, in its report on migrant issues, home ownership did not solve the problems of migrant housing. A 1976 study by the state Office of Migrant Affairs showed that two-thirds of all migrant houses were in poor or very poor condition. A significant number had no indoor toilets, and many were pest-infested.

The fact that a major organization such as the Conference of Churches saw fit to study farm worker issues represented an advance for Texas migrants. In the aftermath of the 1966 melon strike and the national publicity given to Cesar Chavez in California and Edward R. Murrow in Florida, middle-class Texans were becoming sensitive to the problems of migrant farm workers.

## SETBACKS AND CHANGES

At the same time that many problems of migrant workers were coming to public attention, the farm worker unions faced new challenges to their very existence.

In Ohio growers formed three different organizations to combat the influence of FLOC: the Ohio Agricultural Marketing Association, Help Establish Legislative Protection (HELP), and the Farm Labor Advisory Group (FLAG). Each of these groups focused on a particular area of concern: HELP lobbied the state legislature; FLAG recruited workers for an emergency labor pool; and the Marketing Association dealt with the contracts already signed between growers and FLOC. Twelve members of the Marketing Association invalidated their agreements with FLOC by switching to crops other than the ones covered under union contract. New agreements were eventually negotiated but not before FLOC had threatened court action.

In 1970, Cesar Chavez visited Toledo to demonstrate

support for FLOC and ask for continued participation in the grape boycott. In a speech to the membership of FLOC, Chavez summed up the challenge facing both unions: "We want sufficient power to control our own destinies. This is our struggle. It's a lifelong job. The work for social change and against social injustice is never ended."[3]

Chavez spoke from firsthand experience about the never-ending nature of the farm worker's struggle. UFWOC was already in the midst of a battle to keep the gains it had so painstakingly won. By 1970 the boycott had convinced most table grape growers to sign with UFWOC. This victory by a small and poorly financed group of migrant farm workers sent shock waves through the whole of California agribusiness. To keep UFWOC from spreading its influence into other areas and other crops, vegetable growers made an alliance with the Teamsters Union that soon became a threat to UFWOC's very existence.

At that time, the Teamsters were the biggest, richest union in the whole labor movement. They had a reputation for corruption and underworld connections that got them expelled from the AFL-CIO in 1957. Since then, they had become known for "sweetheart" contracts, agreements very favorable to the interests of employers that did little to protect the rights of workers.

Teamster supporters would have argued that their contracts were realistic, whereas UFWOC's were demanding too much too soon. Out of all the controversy over which union had the right to represent migrant farm workers, one fact emerged clearly: employers preferred dealing with the Teamsters. Before the table grape contracts came up for renewal in 1975, UFWOC prepared for a major jurisdictional dispute. Recognizing the need for powerful backing in any such confrontation with the Teamsters, UFWOC merged with the AFL-CIO, becoming a full-fledged member of the nationwide labor organization, and adopted yet another name: the United Farm Workers of America (UFW).

As Cesar Chavez and his staff had feared, UFW lost most of its hard-won contracts as grower after grower defected to the Teamsters. The alliance with AFL-CIO greatly increased UFW's chances of success in opposing the Teamsters, but it brought one unwelcome side effect: the student activists who had helped form the union now felt betrayed by it. In their eyes, Big Labor was as bad as Big Business or Big Government: all were establishment, none could be trusted by activists who remained true to their vision. Many left UFW to champion other, fresher, causes.

With AFL-CIO backing, UFW launched a worldwide boycott of non-UFW grapes, head lettuce, and Gallo wines. By 1975, the boycott was so successful that growers threw their support behind a collective bargaining law for farmworkers, which was currently before the state legislature. The Agricultural Labor Relations Act of 1975 created a five-member board to oversee secret ballot elections, allowing migrant workers to decide whether they wished to be represented by the Teamsters, UFW, or no union at all. According to Associated Press figures, UFW won over 83 percent of those elections and in 1977 negotiated a jurisdictional agreement with the Teamsters that put an end to the dispute between the two unions.

## THE FIGHT IN FLORIDA

In 1972, eastern-stream migrants faced a challenge of their own. A committee of the Florida State Legislature was considering a new right-to-work bill. This proposed law had several provisions that would hurt the union movement among eastern-stream migrants, but most damaging of all was a clause prohibiting hiring halls for migrants. This one factor was dangerous enough to attract the interest of UFW, which sent organizers across the country to mount a strong opposition to the bill. Without hiring halls, migrant farm workers would be at the mercy of often unscrupulous crew leaders.

UFW had long believed that the labor contractor system was inherently bad for farm workers, even when the crew leader himself might be a decent, fair-minded person. The contractor would always be a middleman, making his living by standing between the people who did the hiring and those who did the work. His profit almost always resulted in lower wages for the workers in his crew.

Eliseo Medina, the UFW organizer who headed the Florida project, explained why UFW went to such lengths to defeat the prohibition against hiring halls:

> *The reason a hiring hall is important to us is because of the way people get jobs in agriculture. In Belle Glade, Florida, for instance, workers get up at 3:00 A.M. to look for a job and go to the loading ramp where all the labor contractors park their busses.*
>
> *If there are more workers than jobs, the labor contractors hand pick you just like you were cattle. "You're too fat, you won't be able to bend over" or "You're too old, too skinny, or a known trouble maker." You never know what you're going to be paid, and if you complain about the housing or conditions, you get fired on the spot. The hiring hall changes all this, establishing rules by which people can get jobs without discrimination. And you can't be fired just because a foreman doesn't like you. It provides job protection.*[4]

Medina and his staff organized a letter-writing campaign and arranged for union volunteers to visit state senators and legislators. Out of 120 legislators, UFW talked with 103, and out of 40 senators they contacted 32. Despite all this work, experienced observers of the Florida legislature

believed that passage of the right-to-work bill was a fo_
gone conclusion. They felt that farm workers didn't have
the money or the power to influence lawmakers and rally
public sympathy for their cause.

Then UFW learned of a typhoid epidemic in the labor
camp at Homestead, a city-run facility that had been
called the best migrant camp in the state. The epidemic
peaked at about 280 victims in early March 1973 and was
eventually traced to a tainted water supply. According to
Medina, the epidemic shocked the whole state. How
could this have happened in a wealthy nation with strict
sanitation laws? Those laws should have completely elim-
inated typhoid long ago. Suddenly, people who never
thought about migrant farm workers were outraged and
concerned by the epidemic at Homestead.

While the typhoid outbreak was still fresh in people's
minds, union organizers found a labor contractor named
Joe Brown, who had been keeping twenty-nine farm
workers as slaves. Of those twenty-nine, all were under-
nourished and most were suffering from a variety of mental and physical illnesses. Eliseo Medina got the idea of
taking the enslaved workers to testify before the right-to-
work committee of the state legislature. He believed that
the very existence of these men would be powerful evidence against the labor contractor system. None of the
twenty-nine newly liberated workers was in any condition
to offer testimony in public, so Medina found two workers
who had previously escaped from Joe Brown. They were
willing to appear before the legislative committee and
tell about being kept in chains, beaten for the slightest
infractions of Joe Brown's rules, and denied any sanitary
facilities or health care. The testimony of these men was
so effective that the hiring hall ban failed in committee
by a vote of fifteen to seven.

Because of the UFW Florida project, state officials
began to enforce the Crew Leader Registration Act, so
there would be no recurrence of the Joe Brown incident,

*Haitian family in southern Florida*

and to monitor migrant labor camps for compliance with health and safety codes.

By the end of the seventies, migrant workers all over the country had experienced success and failure, advances and setbacks. Not even the most optimistic among them believed that all their problems would be solved in one swift, dramatic stroke. Change would come slowly, built on the work of people who were idealistic enough to struggle against overwhelming odds and realistic enough to understand that minor, short-term victories could in time add up to long-term improvements in the lives of migrant farm workers everywhere.

# BATALLANDO CON LA VIDA: "I AM STILL STRUGGLING WITH LIFE"

As a response to "how are you?" *batallando con la vida* is roughly equivalent to the American "hanging in there." It is also a good description of the situation facing migrant farm workers in the last quarter of the twentieth century. Though much was accomplished in the sixties and seventies, issues of health and safety, housing, wages, and working conditions continue to be a problem. A 1990 pamphlet on the work of FLOC in Ohio contains the following statement from the American Friends Service Committee: "We have found that, in spite of public concern over the years, the living and working conditions for people in the migrant stream have not improved. . . . Life for the migrant farm worker involves back-breaking work, poor pay, living in rundown housing, contact with dangerous pesticides and exploitation by growers and crew leaders."[1]

## HEALTH AND SAFETY

In a report dated May 29, 1990, the Department of Health and Human Services, Migrant Health Program, gives statistics almost identical to those that appeared in the *Congressional Record* more than twenty years earlier:

> *The infant mortality rate for migrants is 125 percent higher than the national average.*

*The life expectancy of a migrant farmworker is 49 years, as compared to the national average of 75 years. . . . Migrant workers experience substantially higher rates than the general population of accidental injuries, mental health and substance abuse problems, and dental and oral disease.*[2]

Other sources corroborate and expand on these figures. A University of North Carolina study of 543 white, Hispanic, black, and Haitian migrant farm workers showed the rate of tuberculosis among black migrant workers born in the United States to be 300 times higher than the overall U.S. rate. In a press release on April 4, 1991, the researchers said that their results contradicted a 1985 report by the National Centers for Disease Control, which considered tuberculosis an imported problem among farm workers. The North Carolina results "indicate that TB among farmworkers is an occupational problem, not an imported one."[3]

Figures on cancer among migrant workers are equally disturbing to health care professionals. A 1990 FLOC report on midwestern migrants found the rate of skin, lung, colon, and cervical cancer to be 10 times higher among farm workers than in the general population.[4] In California, a 1989 health survey of children in the town of McFarland uncovered a "cancer cluster" involving at least thirteen children, most from poor farm worker families who blamed pesticide exposure for the cancers.

The survey could not confirm or deny that pesticides were to blame for the McFarland cancers. Nonetheless, environmentalists as well as farm workers have become increasingly concerned about the toxic effects of agricultural chemicals. In 1990, this concern translated itself into a $500,000 Congressional appropriation to assess the danger that farm workers face from pesticides. Principal researcher for the study was Dr. Marion Moses, a leading authority on the health of migrant farm workers. To obtain

88

*This photo was taken in a house that shelters
thirty-four people. To this day, many migrant
farm workers live in substandard housing and
have little or no access to health care.*

suitable subjects, Dr. Moses turned to the FLOC in north-
western Ohio. She was able to select four hundred people
whose migrancy pattern was predictable enough to allow
researchers to follow and test them for an entire year.

"We have a toxic agriculture today," Dr. Moses told
an interviewer for the *New York Times*, "and the pressure
for changing it is coming from consumers. . . . I guaran-
tee that if you protect these workers in their workplace,

you'll do much more to protect the consumer in the marketplace."[5]

Rules that do exist to protect migrant workers from pesticide exposure are often ignored, according to farm worker advocacy groups. In November 1989, for example, eighty-five workers were injured in Balm, Florida, when their employer sent them into fields freshly sprayed with an insecticide called phosdrin, which has the same chemical properties as nerve gas. In Texas, a group of migrant workers told of hoeing cabbage while a plane dusted the field with pesticides, and in California, nearly two hundred labor camps were cited in September 1991 for failure to test drinking water to ensure it was free of pesticide residues or other contaminants.

Dangerous as pesticides might be, they cause only a fraction of farm injuries, according to Dr. Marc Schenker of the University of California at Davis. "Traumatic injury is the major problem in California and most of the country," he told a reporter for the Sacramento *Bee*. Dr. Schenker cited figures showing that occupational deaths in California farming average 16 per 100,000 workers— more than double the state average for all workplace deaths. In addition to these fatalities, 22,000 nonfatal injuries are reported each year, making the farm California's deadliest job site.[6] These statistics, along with similar ones from other farming regions, convinced the federal government to establish two Agricultural Health and Safety Centers: one at the University of California, Davis, and another at the University of Iowa. Researchers will study agricultural work hazards and develop equipment and procedures to make the farm a safer place to work.

## HOUSING

On any list of migrant concerns, housing ranks near the top, right along with wages, working conditions, and health hazards. In 1980, a nationwide study found two-thirds of all migrant housing to be substandard. More than a decade later, the situation was largely unchanged and, in many cases, noticeably worse. On September 10, 1991, the *Denver Post* published an article by Alan Gottlieb, calling the farm worker housing situation "a national disaster."

Gottlieb wrote:

> *Migrant housing has always been substandard, but over the past two years, stronger enforcement of federal housing standards . . . has led farmers to close down [their] migrant camps. The farmers aren't legally required to provide housing, so when fines become burdensome, many choose to get out of the housing business. Increasingly, migrant farm workers in Colorado and throughout the nation are being forced to sleep in cars, at campsites, or in substandard private market housing over which the federal government has no regulatory control.*[7]

There are some bright spots in the migrant housing picture—new laws enacted and existing ones enforced. In 1990, Congress passed the National Affordable Housing Act, which provides 360,000 low-income housing units all over the country, extends community development programs, and continues rental assistance programs for migrants.

With help from various farm worker rights groups, such as California's Rural Legal Assistance Foundation, migrants are beginning to stand up for their rights. In July 1991, a group of twenty-four migrant farm workers reported squalid and unhealthful conditions at a Live Oak (northern California) labor camp. When the grower fired those workers, a U.S. district judge issued an order under a 1982 law called the Migrant and Seasonal Agricultural

*Temporary shantytowns, like this one outside
San Diego, are the only shelters some migrants
ever have. In 1990, Congress enacted the
National Affordable Housing Act, to provide
low-income workers with a better place to live.*

Workers Protection Act (AWPA). The grower not only
had to rehire the workers but repair or replace the substandard labor camp.

In another California case, workers who sued under
AWPA were countersued by the grower, who claimed
that it was their fault the camp was substandard. Attorney
Michael Kanz told a reporter for the Sacramento *Bee* that

"it appears . . . this lawsuit is a tactic being used to intimidate those farm workers who have stood up for their rights. The message seems to be: assert your rights to lawful housing and employment conditions and you, too, will be sued."[8]

## WAGES AND WORKING CONDITIONS

In 1982 the Department of Agriculture created the Agricultural Employment Work Group, a team of experts who conducted a survey of working conditions on American farms. The group recommended strategies to reconcile the needs of farm owners with those of farm workers, thereby expanding options for everybody involved in agriculture. These strategies were summarized as follows:

- Improve farm workers' annual income
- Increase productivity and improve efficiency in the utilization of agricultural labor
- Stabilize employment patterns
- Improve the quality of life of agricultural workers
- Improve the quality of agricultural work
- Expand options for self-determination[9]

Migrant farm workers in Texas put this theme of expanded options for all into action long before the Department of Agriculture put it into words. In the summer of 1978, domestic migrants and H-2 (legal alien) workers joined together in a work stoppage that won better wages and working conditions in the melon and onion fields of Presidio, Texas. That action mushroomed into an organizing drive that culminated in February 1979 with the largest farm worker gathering in the history of Texas. The workers set priorities for their organizing efforts and established committees to take the plan to the workers in the fields. In 1981, the new union scored its first legislative victory, a ban on *el cortito*, the short-handled hoe. This was a tremendous moral victory as well as a practical one. By 1984, UFW had forty organizing committees in south Texas, and an office for legislative advocacy in the state capital at Austin. The union achieved another legislative milestone that year when a bill granting Workers' Compensation to farm workers injured on the job was passed.

In Ohio, FLOC developed the Platform for Justice, a three-way negotiating strategy that gave shape and

*Through widespread organizing and careful strategies, farm workers in Texas have steadily gained better work conditions and wages.*

substance to Department of Agriculture ideas about reconciling the needs of all groups involved in farming. According to a union pamphlet,

> to understand how [the Platform for Justice] works, we first have to look at the differing goals and needs of the three primary parties that make up the vegetable industry in the midwest. . . . The corporate processors . . . want skilled crop harvesting to produce the

*grade of vegetable they need for a consistent quality
produced at the lowest possible price. . . . The family
farmers . . . need longer term commitments from the
processors on price, and a skilled, dependable labor
force for the harvest. . . . The farmworkers . . . need
the dignity of a fair wage for a day's work. They
also need . . . the status of workers, not exploited
sharecroppers, with Social Security, Unemployment
Compensation and Workers' Compensation for injuries.''* [10]

Three years after FLOC began using its Platform for
Justice as a foundation for negotiating, workers had
gained 18 percent in wages and seen improvements in
housing and health care. Family farmers had gained guar-
anteed, multiyear contracts, and the processors had experienced a 40 percent increase in productivity measured in
value per harvested acre. Despite these successes in the
eighties and early nineties, much remained to be done.
According to FLOC, the workers and farmers involved
in the platform process represented only 5 percent of the
industry, and the hard-won union contracts covered only
six thousand of the more than one hundred thousand migrant farm workers in Ohio. FLOC's response to the
problem was to broaden its base of action. In the late
eighties, the union began organizing in Michigan and
Illinois and extended member-service programs into Florida and Texas, where the majority of FLOC members
spend the winter months.

   In 1990, both FLOC and UFW made important
agreements that extended their outreach to the thousands
of Mexican nationals who still enter the country each year
to work on U.S. farms. On April 23, 1990, UFW signed
an historic agreement with the government of Mexico,
allowing Mexicans working in the United States to provide medical benefits for their families back home. FLOC

*Up until his death in early 1993, Cesar Chavez's efforts kept the UFW strong and vital in representing the interests of farm workers.*

negotiated a mutual aid pact with SNTOAC, Mexico's largest farm worker union. According to FLOC, "members envision the day when agribusiness cannot threaten to move to the next state, or even overseas, because workers everywhere will be linked with one another in solidarity, for dignity and justice."[11]

In the midst of these advances, familiar problems

continue to occur. In California, the Agricultural Labor Relations Act, which seemed so promising when it was enacted in 1975, was rarely enforced by 1984. According to UFW, "the hard-earned benefits . . . disappeared, and farm workers were forced to endure the horrible conditions that existed before."[12] In response, Cesar Chavez called for yet another boycott of California table grapes, an action that was to last into the nineties, with no end in sight.

On September 12, 1990, the Sacramento *Bee* ran a photo that looked like something straight out of the sixties: Cesar Chavez being arrested for picketing a supermarket that sold California table grapes. In September of the next year, another photo showed Chavez and a group of UFW volunteers picketing a San Francisco television station that had aired a report critical of the union. According to an Associated Press article for September 25, 1991, "The two four-minute segments aired on national television last week, portraying the union and its founder as having abandoned the plight of farm workers. . . . Chavez challenged the report, saying sources backed by growers purposely gave the reporter inaccurate information, including incorrect union membership numbers and fund-raising figures."[13]

In the midst of these controversies, new ethnic groups continue to arrive in the United States, competing with established migrants for available jobs and creating new challenges for unions and community service agencies. Many of these recent arrivals speak regional dialects that outsiders don't understand. In California, Mixtec Indians from the state of Oaxaca in southern Mexico bring abject poverty and their own ancient language into the western migrant stream, while in Florida, workers from the Caribbean have caused a growing number of migrant health centers to become multilingual, offering services in Haitian Creole as well as English and Spanish.

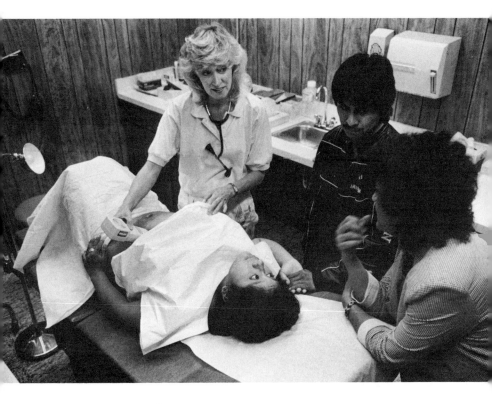

*As migrant workers continue to arrive from Mexico, Haiti, and other Caribbean nations, health care clinics now provide services in Spanish and Creole as well as English.*

In Washington, D.C., a Congressional committee held hearings in the summer of 1991, to determine the extent of migrant farm workers' problems. The findings of that committee echoed a familiar theme, according to Representative Edward Roybal: "Such critical problem areas as an almost complete lack of quality health care, pesticide exposure with little or no regulation, and grossly inadequate family housing are just a few of the inhuman

*Bell pepper picker near Hereford, Texas*

conditions . . . which we have allowed to continue unchallenged."[14]

In the midst of government inquiries and university studies, the hopes and dreams of migrant farm workers in the nineties remain much the same as they have always been: a living wage, a safe workplace, and decent housing for themselves and their families. How and when these goals will be achieved have been the source of much controversy over the years, but all concerned agree on one point: it will not be easy, it will not be quick. In the words of the FLOC activist Sister Pearl McGivney, "Justice in the fields of America is a long row to hoe!"

# SOURCE NOTES

## PROLOGUE: LIVING THE MIGRANT LIFE

1. The stories in this prologue are true but not altogether factual. Names and some nonessential incidents have been changed to protect privacy.

2. Mixtec information comes from a conference, "Oaxacan Migrant Families in Central California," held in Madera under sponsorship of the University of California Cooperative Extension.

3. The data on the vigilante action and conflict between workers and owners in the peach orchards are drawn from news articles published in the Sacramento *Bee* as well as radio and television news broadcasts.

   The material concerning the Kelseyville walnut harvest and the case history of the Gonzales family come from interviews by the author.

4. Material on the south Texas colonias comes from studies done by the Texas Department of Human Services.

## CHAPTER ONE: EARLY HISTORY AND ECONOMICS OF MIGRANT LABOR

1. Childe, V. Gordon, *Man Makes Himself* (New York: Oxford Univ. Press, 1939). Reprinted in *Exploring*

*The Ways Of Mankind*, Walter Goldschmidt, ed. (New York: Holt, Rinehart and Winston), p. 139.

2. Sowell, Thomas, *Ethnic America: A History* (New York: Basic Books, 1981), p. 27.

3. Schlebecker, John T., *Whereby We Thrive: A History of American Farming, 1607–1972* (Ames, Iowa: Iowa State University Press, 1975), p. 192.

4. McWilliams, Carey, *Factories in the Fields*, 3rd ed. (Santa Barbara: Peregrine Publishers, 1971), p. 130.

5. McCunn, Ruthanne Lum, *An Illustrated History of the Chinese In America* (San Francisco: Design Enterprises, 1979), p. 43.

## CHAPTER TWO: MIGRANT LABOR AND THE GREAT DEPRESSION

1. Allen, Frederick Lewis, *Since Yesterday* (New York: Harper & Row, 1939), pp. 196–214.

2. Shannon, David A., *The Great Depression* (Englewood Cliffs, N.J.: Prentice-Hall, 1960), p. 59.

3. Lusk, R. D., article in *Saturday Evening Post*, August 13, 1938; reprinted in *Rural America*, Suzanne Freemon and Morrow Wilson, eds. (New York: H. W. Wilson, 1976), p. 91.

4. Horan, James D., *The Desperate Years: A Pictorial History of the Thirties* (New York: Crown Publishers, 1962), p. 163.

5. Neuberger, Richard L., *Our Promised Land* (New York: MacMillan, 1938); reprinted in *Rural America*, Suzanne Freemon and Morrow Wilson, eds. (New York: H. W. Wilson, 1976), p. 95.

6. Ibid.

7. Steinbeck, John, *The Grapes Of Wrath* (New York: Viking Press, 1939; Penguin Books ed. 1976), p. 118.

8. Ibid., p. 448–49.

## CHAPTER THREE: HANDS FROM MEXICO

1. Galarza, Ernesto, *Merchants of Labor: the Mexican Bracero Story* (Charlotte/Santa Barbara: McNally & Loftin, 1964), p. 17.

2. Oliveira, Victor J., *Trends in the Hired Farm Work Force: 1945–1987* (Washington, D.C., U.S. Dept. of Agriculture Bulletin No. 561, 1989), p. 7.

3. Galarza, p. 48.

4. Oliveira, p. 7.

5. Kelley, Willard F., *Immigration and Naturalization Service Reporter* (Washington, D.C.: U.S. Department of Justice, January, 1954), p. 39.

6. Galarza, p. 57.

## CHAPTER FOUR: A NEW FEELING IN THE LAND

1. Coles, Robert, *Migrants, Sharecroppers, Mountaineers* (Vol. 2 of Children of Crisis). (Boston: Little, Brown, 1971), p. 427.

2. Ibid., p. 95.

3. Matthiessen, Peter, *Sal Si Puedes: Cesar Chavez and the New American Revolution* (New York: Random House, 1969), p. 69.

4. Horowitz, George D., and Fusco, Paul, *La Causa: The California Grape Strike* (New York: Collier Books, 1970), p. 31.

5. Levy, Jacques, *Cesar Chavez: Autobiography of La Causa* (New York: W. W. Norton, 1975), p. 75.

6. Terkel, Studs, *Working: People Talk About What They Do All Day Long and How They Feel About What They Do* (New York: Pantheon Books, 1972) p. 181.

7. Galarza, Ernesto, *Merchants of Labor: The Mexican Bracero Story* (Charlotte/Santa Barbara: McNally and Loftin, 1964), p. 95.

8. Levy, p. 129.

## CHAPTER FIVE: THE FOUNDING OF A UNION

1. Galarza, Ernesto, *Merchants of Labor: The Mexican Bracero Story* (Charlotte/Santa Barbara: McNally and Loftin, 1964), p. 253.

2. Levy, Jacques, *Cesar Chavez: Autobiography of La Causa* (New York: W. W. Norton, 1975), p. 162.

3. Ibid., p. 176.

4. Constitution of the United Farm Workers of America, 1988.

## CHAPTER SIX: VIVA LA CAUSA!

1. Levy, Jacques, *Cesar Chavez: Autobiography of La Causa* (New York: W. W. Norton, 1975), p. 184.

2. Ibid., p. 296.

3. Valez-Cox, Juanita, ''The Starr County Farmworkers' Strike of 1966–67: A Demonstration of Elitist Control of Power'' (Unpublished paper, December 7, 1988), p. 10.

## CHAPTER SEVEN: TAKING THE LONG VIEW

1. "A Factual Rebuttal to the Farmers' and Growers' Attack on Our Nation's Farmworkers," *Congressional Record* (Vol. 114, No. 169, Oct. 11, 1968).

2. Coles, Robert, *Migrants, Sharecroppers, Mountaineers* (Vol. 2 of *Children of Crisis*) (Boston: Little, Brown, 1971), p. 511.

3. Farm Labor Organizing Committee, "FLOC: Ten Years of Struggle" (Toledo, Ohio, 1990). Pamphlet.

4. Levy, p. 454.

## CHAPTER EIGHT: "BATALLANDO CON LA VIDA"

1. Farm Labor Organizing Committee, "For Justice" (Toledo, Ohio, 1990). Pamphlet.

2. Migrant Health Program, "Access of Migrant and Seasonal Farm Workers to Medicaid Covered Health Care Services" (Washington, D.C.: Migrant Health Program Report, May 29, 1990).

3. "High TB Rate for Black Farm Workers," Sacramento *Bee*, April 4, 1991.

4. Farm Labor Organizing Committee, "FLOC Platform for Justice" (Toledo, Ohio, 1990). Report.

5. Schneider, Keith, "Migrant Worker Group Is Subject of Wide Study," *The New York Times*, August 19, 1990.

6. Brank, Glenn, "Doing Right(s): A Low Profile Attorney Fights the Battle of Farmworkers," Sacramento *Bee*, September 9, 1990.

7. Gottlieb, Alan, "Migrant Housing a U.S. Emergency, Council Says," *Denver Post*, Sept. 10, 1991.

8. Breton, Marcos, "Judge Orders Repairs at Camp for Farm Workers," Sacramento *Bee*, June 12, 1991.

9. United States Department of Agriculture, Agricultural Employment Work Group, "Agricultural Labor in the 1980's: A Survey and Recommendations," Washington, D.C., 1982.

10. Farm Labor Organizing Committee: "FLOC's Platform for Justice: A Win-Win Experience" (Toledo, Ohio, 1990), p. 2. Pamphlet.

11. Farm Labor Organizing Committee, "For Justice: Farm Labor Organizing Committee" (Toledo, Ohio, 1990). Pamphlet.

12. United Farm Workers of America, "Biographical Sketch of Cesar Chavez." (Keene, Calif., 1990). Pamphlet.

13. Associated Press, "Report on Chavez Union Hit," Sacramento *Bee*, Sept. 25, 1991.

14. Micoy, Laura. "Farm Workers Outline Problems: House Committee Hears of Pesticide Exposure, Dilapidated Housing," Sacramento *Bee*, July 18, 1991.

# FOR FURTHER READING

Coles, Robert. *Children Of Crisis Vol. II: Migrants, Sharecroppers, and Mountaineers.* Boston: Little, Brown, 1973.

Gonzales, Juan L. *Mexican-American Farm Workers: The California Agricultural Industry.* Westport, CT: Praeger Publishers, 1985.

Gorman, Carol. *America's Farm Crisis.* New York: Franklin Watts, 1987.

Greene, Laura O. *Child Labor: Then and Now.* New York: Franklin Watts, 1992.

Kahn, Kathy. *Fruits Of Our Labor.* New York: G.P. Putnam's Sons, 1982.

Levy, Jacques E. *Cesar Chavez: Autobiography of La Causa.* New York: W.W. Norton & Co., 1975.

Matthiessen, Peter. *Sal Si Puedes: Cesar Chavez and the New American Revolution.* New York: W.W. Norton & Co., 1969.

Meltzer, Milton. *Bread and Roses: The Struggle of American Labor.* New York: NAL, 1985.

Steinbeck, John. *The Grapes Of Wrath.* New York: Viking Press, 1939.

Time-Life Books. *This Fabulous Century: 1930–1940.* New York: Time-Life Books, 1988.

# INDEX

Page numbers in *italics* refer to photographs.